Parables and Encounters

Temi Fagade

Parables and Encounters

Email: temifagade@gmail.com
ISBN: 978-1-911312-05-5

Published by: Lacepoint Publishing
www.lacepoint.ie | Email: services@lacepoint.ie
Tel: +353 1 504 3013

Dedication

I'm giving this to You, Precious Holy Spirit. I relish greatly and celebrate the diverse encounters I have experienced with and in You. This Christian walk seems so easy as You show up time and time again thereby affirming my faith. Ah! What would I do without You, Sweet Holy Spirit? I truly celebrate and cherish Your presence within me. Thank you for rebukes and corrections, timely guidance, inspirations, revelations, quickening, help and all You do for me.

Also to every child of God, every remnant in all nations who truly are following the leading of the Holy Spirit and as many as are desirous to hear His voice, have an intimate walk with Him and surrender totally to His leading for their lives.

Acknowledgement

I acknowledge the husband of my youth, Omotayo Fagade, thank you for believing in me, for your unwavering support at all times and for making room for the full expression of God`s mandate in my life. You remain my number one critic and yet my number one fan!

To our three covenant blessings: David, Deborah and Mateuzinho; quivers you three will always be and surely, you will all stand and contend with the enemy at the gates. I am grateful to you all for your understanding and loyal support during times I had to devote myself more to praying, studying and writing. Thank you for all for cheering me on, for consenting to sharing some of our personal experiences in encouraging others and for believing in this project; indeed, we make a formidable team.

To my parents, Mr. Theophilus & Mrs Adenike Ayeni, thank you for the bond of family, thank you for all you do. I am blessed to have you both as the channel through which the Lord brought me to this world. Pillars you two are to me.

To my three siblings Tolu, Tayo and Dayo, I can always depend on you as Aaron, Ur and Joshua to lift up my arms for victory till all Amalekites are completely smitten.

Warm appreciation to my second Father, Mr. Adedamola Afolabi Adams, thank you sir for painstakingly going through the manuscript. Your ever encouraging words and prayers sure mean much. I can always badge in on you anytime and be rest assured of that fatherly succour.

My indebtedness goes to many individuals in the faith and bodies of Christ who have at one time or the other contributed in no small measure to nurturing the Holy seed that was birthed in me at salvation.

I have been nourished, discipled and privileged to serve in many ministries as I relocated to various locations at different phases of my life. Worthy of mention are the Student Christian Movement University of Ibadan, Glory Tabernacle Ministries Ibadan, The Redeemed Christian Church of God, Okota –Lagos and Aberdeen Scotland, World Alive Ministries, Port Harcourt, The Men of Issachar Vision, Brazil, the Winners Chapel, Worldwide and Nehemiah Troop Prayer Ministry under the lead servant, Rev. Raeni Bankole; I appreciate you deeply.

I cannot but give special recognition to a father of fathers, one whom the Lord has used to ignite the faith fire in me in the person of Bishop David Olaniyi Oyedepo. My connection to your ministry was divinely orchestrated. I follow you as you follow Christ sir. Thank you for obeying the Liberation Mandate. Respect Papa!

On this book project, your support has been overwhelming Isekhua Evborokhai, I can't forget when you called me years back from Ireland to ask when I would publish a book and offered to help in any way possible; thank you brother, we sure have come a long way. And of a truth, your helpers shall not be few.

I acknowledge RiriOghene Onosu, my little mentee, having you watch my back and cheering me on. Thank you Miss Riri!

I am grateful to many dear friends and I sure have them not a few! If I were to include all names herein, time and space would not suffice! You all already know I have a special place in my heart for each individual I call a friend.

Lord Jesus, again, I celebrate Your acts in my life. Not sure I can ever comprehend why Your love and mercy keeps flowing towards me but I want to shout it on the roof tops that I'm grateful and owe everything to Your finished work on the cross for me. I consciously remain

Your bond servant and continually, I pledge my allegiance to You, the Lamb of God.

Contents

Also by this author

Not A Stranger to Storms *is an inspirational piece revealing testimonies of God`s faithfulness in aspects of healings, overcoming trials of parenting, conception amongst other challenging situations. Absolute trust in God for all whims in life`s sojourn are presented in story format herein and as such, makes this book of testimonies a must read for all and sundry*

Foreword

Does God still speak to His people? Does the Holy Spirit still provide guidance and leading to God's children or is it a thing of the past? Is God's voice and guidance only available to the clergy or to all of His children?

Whatever your answer to these questions may be, Temi, in this her second book: "Parables and Encounters" reveals to us; from first-hand experiences with the Holy Spirit that God is still very much in the business of speaking, leading, guiding and directing the affairs of His children today as He did in Bible days.

God uses various means to reach out and speak to His people though His providence; sovereignly working behind the scenes, even when we are not aware of it, to work all things after the counsel of His will. Our everyday lives are surrounded by the allegorical parables of hidden symbols and encounters. He takes delight in speaking to us through our daily encounters so that we can be enlightened in conducting our affairs in the present and in the future.

Each chapter of "Parables and Encounters" opens with a very well-articulated short story comprising either a personal revelational encounter with the Holy Spirit or a real life, deep and rich encounter worth learning from. It is important to learn from the experiences of others because those who do not learn from history and the experiences of others are bound to repeat the same errors, howbeit with grievous repercussions.

Temi has carefully narrated and intricately woven these stories and encounters into the book to carefully guide the reader into the deep, indelible encounters and experiences she'd had with the Holy Spirit. Many of these experiences she shared were received in the form of parables laced with mysteries left to be unravelled by her. And the unravelling provided guidance and assurance in many of her life's decisions.

In this book, Temi has maintained her original uncomplicated, conversational and easy to read writing style that keeps the reader captivated from start to finish. She concludes each chapter with eight Bible and faith based prayers; engaging the reader and ensuring that the reading of the book is more of an experience than a ritual.

This book lucidly offers profound insight into the author`s personal life and encounters which bears out some incredible testimonies of what a believer can accomplish.

"Parables & Encounters" has enough sparks to light a thousand fires in every reader's heart as they confront various circumstances common to all on a daily basis.
I recommend this book unreservedly to all eager to follow and experience God in a more intimate manner.

Dr Sola Oduwole
Pastor, RCCG SA Province 2
Cape Town, South Africa

Preface

An evidence that God's presence is dwelling in a person is that such an individual is guided by the Holy Spirit. That is what Romans 8:14 teaches us: *"For as many as are led by the Spirit of God, these are sons of God."*

Being guided by God means to hear His voice in our conscience, through His word, our thoughts, even in our dreams or through prophetic words He might speak to us. The fear of God is an anchor that ensures the Holy Spirit keeps us in His commandments and path

This leading of the Holy Spirit is the greatest asset I have come to treasure in this Christian walk with the Lord. His leading ensures guidance in the murky waters of life. Often times His voice brings rebuke especially at points of erring; a leading that continually aligns me correctly on this narrow path.

This journal summarized some experiences and intimate encounters of God's gracious dealings with me as I learnt to recognize, understand and follow His leading through His voice in my heart, in visions, revelations and dreams.

In those encounters, my attention was always sharply caught!

Some of the things He taught me through those indelible encounters are very relatable to all and sundry. Most came like parables that formed a bedrock for deeper search and meditation in God's word; and by the help of the Holy Spirit, unravelled its mysteries and received interpretation as it applied to me. These indelible encounters; experiences that birthed precise direction, certainty and efficiency from various mountains of encounters with Him, I have shared in the form of stories in this journal.

It was not uncommon for Jesus to speak and teach using parables to His followers and He further granted them access to the mystery therein in a bid to understand what the Spirit was saying per time. He admonished them that they had access to understanding kingdom mysteries. He answered and said to them, *"Because it has been given to you to know the mysteries of the kingdom of heaven, but to them it has not been given," (Matt 13: 11).*

It is God's plan for each of us to hear His voice. It is not just for a certain select group of people with "special gifts". The level to which we receive instructions from the Holy Spirit depends on our ability to hear God's voice. Aren't you glad that He also promised that His

Holy Spirit would be sent to teach us all things? In first John chapter 2 the Bible says:
"But ye have an anointing from the Holy one, and ye know all things" (1 John 2 verse 20 NKJV).

The anointing speaks to us and brings revelation from God's word to our life. The spirit man of every regenerated heart has been designed to hear God or other voices in the spirit realm.

I therefore submit that receiving and understanding God's leading is a crucial factor for any believer to make progress and impact in this faith walk with the Lord in the days we live in. He said His own disciples would recognise and follow His voice. *"My sheep hear My voice, and I know them, and they follow Me"* (John 10:27).

I earnestly pray that your heart will truly be ministered to as you glean through the pages of this book. While we all may not individually undergo same encounters; and since this book will not pretend to make an exhaustive detail in all aspects, we are being reminded basically that we must consciously pay attention to what the Spirit is saying to the church for ***what He says to one, He says to all!*** Mark 13:37.
Shalom!

CHAPTER ONE

The Messy Kitchen

"The program is all day on Saturday so I'll be away till evening; can I request you and the kids do the shopping for the month that day? We really have run out of stock on many things in the house." I said.

And before he could respond I continued;

"I will make the list of all items we need, the quantity to buy and specify where you pick them, most will be from Costco anyway."

He simply responded "ok" in a smooth lively voice

"And you can get your kids their favourite Pepperoni pizza on your way back too." I added.

He gave an "Ok" as he typed away on his computer

It was one Tuesday evening in the summer of 2007 in the city of Aberdeen, Scotland; one of the few years in which summer was reasonably warm or better put, when summer was "really" summer. Even though it didn't last for long, we maximized it while it lasted.
We chatted about a few other things before retiring for the night.
"Lord, thank You!" I muttered to myself.

With monthly shopping plans out of the way, I could focus on plans for our women's meeting at the church that coming Saturday.
Saturday came, a beautiful, glorious day it was. Having made breakfast for my family while they were all still in bed, I set out early for the full day women's program in church.

The guest speaker was an elderly woman all the way from London. Such an embodiment of meekness she was. Soft spoken, amiable with a matronly air all around her. She oozed out so much warmth.
My Pastor's wife had introduced all members of the women's executive to her.
At my turn, she said: "this is Sis Temi, she's our treasurer and she does such a good job at it."
"Ah! Treasurer? I love treasurers, she should be my best friend." Responded the guest speaker; tongue in cheek.

We all laughed as I took in all about her, not only was she amiable but even her simple appearance spoke volumes.
Her grey dress was Victorian
Pink high-end flat shoes in suede
With a luscious matching silk scarf on her neck
"Expensive" I thought to myself
Her mild perfume was a combo of lemon zest and strawberry.
She sure made an impression on me
And then we settled in to start the meeting.

The attendance was amazingly great, full house it was and a higher percentage of participants were tardy too. From the worship to the loaded prayer sessions, we felt God in our midst. There was so much grace to supplicate personally and intercede for our homes.

The messages shared at the two sessions by our guest speaker were inspirational and deep. I would have termed one a message and other a sermon. We were inspired, instructed, rebuked and challenged to seek God at a deeper depth. In all simplicity and sincerity, we received instructions at the Lord's feet. Truly we were fed! Not forgetting to mention that we snacked and dined at different intervals too.

The meeting ended well after 6.00pm that Saturday.
As I drove home after dropping a few sisters on my way, I was grateful to God for that time spent in His presence.

I arrived home well before the sun set. Aberdeen summer ensured I got home before it was dark.
As I unlocked the door to enter through the front door, a funny smell welcomed me. I wondered what and where that came from.
I went straight into the kitchen and met a shocking view. I took it all in a minute.
To say my kitchen was in a mess would be an understatement! I mean real mess! They had done the shopping alright; but groceries, cartons, plastic bags, littered everywhere. Even the meat and poultry purchased had defrosted and had started dripping blood on the floor!

My first reaction was to scream; but I restrained myself. Glancing in the sitting room direction, my husband and our two kids were obviously enjoying themselves. They were glued to the TV watching one of their favourite shows: "Are you smarter than a 10-year old?"

"Welcome Mommy, how was your program?"
"We got everything on the shopping list you made." my husband furnished.
"Fine, thank you." I replied quietly and started unpacking and storing things away.
By the time I finished cleaning up, I retired upstairs for a shower and to bed thereafter. Not a word to my family as I went upstairs.
Sure it had been a long day and what a way to end it.

I was exhausted but could feel a volcano about to erupt in me
So the man of the house finally came upstairs. Oblivious of my feelings, he chatted on while I responded to all conversations coldly.
In monosyllables, came my responses.
I was boiling within me.
He finally noticed I wasn't so forthcoming and asked what was wrong;
"Everything ok with you?"
My response must have hit him as a rude shock
He was visibly surprised as I continued:
"What would it have cost you people to arrange the things you bought?"
"Should the meat have been left to defrost and drip blood all over the kitchen? The refrigerator and freezer weren't locked you know. Even the kids know where to store things, all you needed was to have told them to do it."
With my voice raised, I ranted on and on.
He opened his mouth to speak but changed his mind.
And silence ensued
It lingered while I waited
Silence
Thick
Suffocating
Silence
Then he finally spoke up in a low tone
"And you just came back from church. You've been in church, in God's presence all day."

That melted me. More like hitting me with a force of rude awakening. I chided myself for being so forthcoming in the first place. However, I held on to my opinion.
And that was it.
Silent treatment activated.
To your tents, O Israel.
Sharing a bed yet we became strangers.
I turned to my side of the wall and he did the same.
Despite my anger, I was exhausted and in no distant time, settled in and slept off.

Early hours of the following Sunday morning, around 4 a.m. or so, I suddenly woke up and felt uneasy. I wondered what could be wrong with me. Why this sudden low feeling?
As I shut my eyes again to resume my sleep, I heard the words in my spirit "***add to your faith virtue***".
It was a very loud and distinct voice within.
I wondered what that was all about. I decided to check it out in my Bible. And so I read 2 Peter 1:5-9

*"But also for this very reason, giving all diligence, **add to your faith virtue**, to virtue knowledge, to knowledge self-control, to self-control perseverance, to perseverance godliness, to godliness brotherly kindness, and to brotherly kindness love. For if these things are yours and abound, you will be neither barren nor unfruitful in the knowledge of our Lord Jesus Christ. For he who lacks these things is short sighted, even to blindness, and has forgotten that he was cleansed from his old sins." Emphasis mine*

I needed no interpreter!
The very words "add to your faith, virtue" literally lifted out of the passage and jumped at me.
That was a word of rebuke for me.
Friends, those words broke my heart completely.
Call it chastisement, call it correction but it was strong.
In other words, the Spirit of God was saying that the faith I was professing with all my religious activities displayed no virtue.
The New International Version calls it *goodness* while New Living Translation refers to it as *moral goodness*. Call it integrity, call it strength of character. Whatever name you call it; it simply meant that my behaviour or reaction that night wasn't consistent with the faith I was professing.

With deep contrition, I asked the Lord to have mercy and help me. And then, I apologised to my husband. I must have apologised to my husband severally. I became so sober that period as I saw my helplessness. I saw myself lacking in virtue. A lack likened to not having a "yellow dress suit" in one's dressing closet; by the way, yellow is a colour that most women tend not to favour in theirs. And if my relationship with the Lord was likened to a dressing closet, virtue was conspicuously missing the exact same way I practically lacked that colour in my physical closet!

For any fruitful growth in Christ, I must grow beyond the level of having faith! Strength of character must be attained as I yield to His instructions revealed from the knowledge of scriptures or as the Spirit prompts me. I must be willing to expose my life to the scan of His words and trust Him to help me effect changes where needs be.

For once, I realised God was interested in every minute detail of my life. It is pertinent that my reaction to people, issues and circumstances be consistent with His words irrespective of how I was treated. In essence, integrity of character must be in place.

I had a mental picture of me in conversation with someone who made derogatory remarks at me, the Holy Spirit was present though unseen. While the person wounded me with words, I responded gently and could imagine the third party in the person of the Holy Spirit applauding my response. But this was not the case the night before. My response would have without a doubt wounded and displeased Him.

Truth be told in retrospect; I should have given details about storing away the items purchased rather than assuming they would know all. I could also have excused them based on the fact that they wanted me to come sort things my way.

I dreaded hearing any further "voice" lest I receive such rebuke again. Not that we haven't had other issues as a couple thereafter but that incident left an indelible mark in my heart.

If my character does not match the faith I profess, religion rather than spirituality may be ruling.

God however is much more interested in building my character than bequeathing me with wealth. The strength of my character means a lot to God. It carries so much weight before Him.

Colossians 3 verse 12 says:

"Therefore, as the elect of God, holy and beloved, put on tender mercies, kindness, humility, meekness, longsuffering;" (NKJV)

In explaining further my stand on this view, let me try to distinguish between religiosity and spirituality using this scripture and making certain analogies in shedding more light.

If the devil was to appear as a snake, a dragon or lion, I may be scared but I won't be deceived. However, we know he comes like an angel of light.

*"And no wonder! **For Satan himself transforms himself into an angel of light."** (2 Corinthians 11 verse 14 NKJV) Emphasis mine*

He doesn't give us "big errors" or come preaching obvious sins or unrighteousness. Instead, to lead astray, he simply and slightly dents the truth; that is what has led to the proliferation of various forms of religion today as well as the various versions of the Christian faith. He knows that as small as a degree shift away from the original course ultimately leads to miles and miles away from one's original destination!

In the same vein, a full bottle of poison is not necessarily required to kill someone; a few drops in a glass of juice or water is harmful enough and can be effective especially when such drops are repeatedly added to the juice or water over and again.

As a Christian, it is very important that you can distinguish between religiosity and spirituality. The former is human while the lätter is divine. A major difference between the two is that true spirituality explains a regenerated heart.

A regenerated heart is one that is continuously malleable in the hands of the Holy Spirit; not a one-time fix or a short-term process. But a heart that is open to being remoulded daily as we attain the very image of Christ. This is by far the most important of all.

A religious heart; based on rules, regulations and traditions on the other hand is only capable of giving a form of godliness; which by no means brings you to Christ as it is only an outward show. So, irrespective of a man's denomination and religious associations, it is pertinent to come to personal faith in Christ.

The Pharisees were religious; they obeyed every external law from synagogue attendance, to vigils and fasts; tithing to the letter, giving to the poor, evangelising, etc. but **they were not devoted to Christ in their hearts**. It is only the heart that has the capacity and inner strength to will a change from old habits and way of living, not the mind. A Gospel that is received in the mind and not the heart will still permit me to do whatever pleases me.

There is something about the heart! Can it be that it is bound closest to our Spirit? Because, only the heart can truly repent and have a change of attitude.

"For with the heart one believes unto righteousness*, and with the mouth confession is made unto salvation. (Romans 10 verse 10 NKJV) Emphasis mine*

Details about the subject of a regenerated heart goes beyond the scope of this book. As we daily walk with the Lord and yield to His Spirit, light will be shed on aspects of our lives where we individually need His help. Just like if all the deeds of Jesus were to be recorded one by one, even the world itself would not contain the books that would be written; John 21 verse 45.

Religiosity is insidious! Religion remains an alternative offered to many by the devil in a bid to make them believe they are "fine" with God.
The Pharisees for instance, believed they were following God; but their beliefs just like many of today were rooted in philosophy, ethics and some cultural doctrines made by men and these would never produce a regenerated heart.
They sought honour for themselves, loved money in their hearts, lived for themselves, cherished the praise and opinion of men **but the inner power to live godly lives was missing!**

*"**having a form of godliness but denying its power**. And from such people turn away!" (2 Timothy 3 verse 5 NKJV) Emphasis mine*

If I fast but cannot control my tongue, then I deny the power therein. I may be ordained in a ministry, have a reputation of being holy but deep inside, I'm empty. The approval of man before heaven has never been about his church title or ordination.

I can do inspiring write-ups and comment beautifully on every social media without real communion with His Spirit. So, eloquence and gifting are not seals of spirituality.

A consistent upward look at God keeps a spiritual person humble such that he even hides his good deeds from the eyes of men. If I'm okay with the praises of men rather than focus on what God thinks of me, then I'm a Pharisee. The urge to please or impress men made king Saul to offer that spiritual barbecue even when it was obvious God was the one delaying him (1 Samuel 13).

"As for Saul, he was still in Gilgal, and all the people followed him trembling. Then he waited seven days, according to the time set by Samuel. But Samuel did not come to Gilgal; and the people were scattered from him. So Saul said, "Bring a burnt offering and peace offerings here to me." And he offered the burnt offering. Now it happened, as soon as he had finished presenting the burnt offering, that Samuel came; and Saul went out to meet him, that he might greet him. And Samuel said, "What have you done?" ***Saul said, "When I saw that the people were scattered from me, and that you did not come within the days appointed, and that the Philistines gathered together at Michmash, then I said, 'The Philistines will now come down on me at Gilgal, and I have not made supplication to the Lord.' Therefore, I felt compelled, and offered a burnt offering."*** *And Samuel said to Saul, "You have done foolishly. You have not kept the commandment of the Lord your God, which He commanded you. For now, the Lord would have established your kingdom over Israel forever. But now your kingdom shall not continue. The Lord has sought for Himself a man after His own heart, and the Lord has commanded him to be commander over His people, because you have not kept what the Lord commanded you. (1 Samuel 13 verse 7-14 NKJV) Emphasis mine*

Saul demonstrated a stand that he would rather keep the praises of the people rather than obey God's principle. This is a mere mark of a very religious heart.

If I can prepare beautiful sermons but relate carelessly to my spouse, then I'm still superficial. We call you blessed if your family members can truly testify to your faith.

If I serve in church but care less about personal sanctification, my spirituality stands to be questioned. Only services offered unto God from sanctified hearts are truly acceptable

If I'm only interested in the letter and do not relate with the Spirit behind the letter, I'm still far from the real deal (John 6:63)

"It is the Spirit who gives life; the flesh profits nothing. The words that I speak to you are spirit, and they are life." (John 6 verse 63 NKJV)

If I'm full of church activities without personal fellowship in His presence perhaps I'm still playing religiosity. A regenerated heart yearns for communion with God's Spirit always.

While we may please men, a true spiritual man is interested in honouring God and God alone. Again, living a godly life is more important than attending meetings. It is all about priority. Without a life personally devoted to Christ in communion in and out of church, I'm just another number in the church.

Church meetings and gatherings should further help to fine tune, reinforce or refresh my spiritual walk and that's why church meetings are called "service". Such meetings service me. We attend church meetings for fresh impact.

Being spiritual is an attitude of the heart and that should be my goal in life. Spiritual people receive God's praise. Jesus lived to please God and not for men's opinion.

However, it takes determination not to live for men's praise. If we are determined to seek and please Him, His Spirit will show us the "how" and grant the inner power to truly live for Him. It is He that gives "the power" to be called sons of God. In other words, He supplies help in any and every aspect of our lives such that we can truly live for Him.

"But as many as received Him, to them He gave the right to become children of God, to those who believe in His name." (John 1 verse 12 NKJV)

A spiritual man studies the word of God and also allows the word to "study" him. When a man truly looks at God from the light of His words, light shines on all unconscious sins in his life. This should actually lead to such an individual being encouraged.

Receiving a word of rebuke from the word of God or from that audible voice in my conscience on any matter needing correction is best likened to being bruised. I however imagine a plant been pruned so it can grow and produce better fruits. It is always a privilege when the Spirit of God corrects me though never palatable initially. Such, rebukes have always made me better in the long run.

One of the baits of the devil with which he deceives many is through the half-truth given as definition of grace, an abuse of grace. The devil would like to hold many down, as such, he has fed many with the lie that when they act contrary to God's words, grace will speak and always cover them. It is true we were all saved by grace but beyond our salvation, the effect (or purpose) of grace is applicable in our walk as we grow onto perfection in our walk.

Put it this way, many believe they have been justified by grace and that grants them access to God's Kingdom despite what they do or how they live their lives; this is erroneous!

This misconception has kept many in the same spot for ages without any spiritual growth or fruits to show.

*"**What shall we say then? Shall we continue in sin that grace may abound? Certainly not!** How shall we who died to sin live any longer in it? Or do you not know that as many of us as were baptized into Christ Jesus were baptized into His death? Therefore, we were buried with Him through baptism into death, that just as Christ was raised from the dead by the glory of the Father, even so we also should walk in newness of life." (Rom 6 verse 1-4 NKJV) Emphasis mine*

The essence of grace is to help us live holy. (Titus 2 verses 11 & 12),

"For the grace of God that brings salvation has appeared to all men, teaching us that, denying ungodliness and worldly lusts, we should live soberly, righteously, and godly in the present age," (Titus 2 verses 11 & 12 NKJV)

Grace is supplied to help us achieve what we as ordinary mortals can't attain. Grace is not a license to continually dwell sin. Grace supplies the winds beneath our wings when we need to fly. Grace is progressive and increases according to the knowledge of God we know.

*"**Grace and peace be multiplied to you in the knowledge of God and of Jesus our Lord,** as His divine power has given to us all things that pertain to life and godliness, through the knowledge of Him who called us by glory and virtue, by which have been given to us exceedingly great and precious promises, that through these you may be partakers of the divine nature,*

having escaped the corruption that is in the world through lust." (2 Peter 1verse 2-4) Emphasis mine

And so, I must grow, adding to my faith virtue, to virtue knowledge, to knowledge self-control, to self-control perseverance, to perseverance godliness.

In the Interim, shall we pray whole heartedly?

1. Father, in the name of Jesus, I thank you for sending Your word my way today. I'm grateful for an encounter through this chapter. Thank you for calling my attention to this issue of living above religiosity. Take all the glory in Jesus' name.

2. Lord, I come with a heart of repentance today, for every act of religiosity, hypocrisy, falsehood, I ask that You have mercy on me O Lord. Please forgive me. You said a broken and a contrite spirit You will not despise (Psalm 51 verse 17). Let the blood of Jesus wash me thoroughly from all such acts in Jesus' name.

3. Lord above self, let me live daily to please You. My focus will not be to please men or seek honour or approval like king Saul. Let me find grace and acceptance in Your sight. Help me to daily walk; being led by Your Spirit concerning every action I take. I enforce Your grace in living above the old nature. By Your grace, I subdue the flesh, the old nature in Jesus' name.

4. Father, I ask, let the beauty of Jesus truly be seen in me. I ask that You open my eyes to every weakness I need to overcome. Help me Lord; of myself I can do nothing. You said to as many as receive You, You have given the power to be called the children of God. (John 1 verse 12); cause that power within me to come alive, help me to detest everything that You detest. Help me to desist from all acts that do not bring You glory in Jesus' mighty name.

5. Lord, open Your word to me as I read. Let Your Spirit give me life, grant me the revelational knowledge of Your word. That the eyes of my understanding be enlightened in Jesus' name. (Ephesians 1 verse 18.) Let understanding come for me via Your word in Jesus' name. That Your word may truly be a light unto my feet and a lamp unto my path in Jesus' name. (Psalm 119 verse 105)

6. Father, by Your grace, I will honour and sanctify You with all of my heart. I will not just offer lip service. (Isaiah 29 verse 13). Make me a true worshipper. Help me to seek You in spirit and in truth; in Jesus' name (John 4 verse 23). As I offer the sacrifice of my lips, cause my heart to be near and in alignment with every word that proceed from my mouth. My heart will not be far from You in Jesus' mighty name. (Matthew 15 verse 8)

7. Lord, purge me of any and every doctrinal error that I've always believed. Purge me of any false doctrines that may poison my spiritual life. Deliver me from every cultural and ancestral belief that still hold me bound. Open my eyes and understanding to the truth. Lead me to the truth that I might be free indeed in Jesus name (John 8 verse 32). I declare that my heart is established by grace through faith in the name of Jesus. (Hebrews 13 verse 9)

8. Father in the name of Jesus, I declare that I add to my faith virtue. Unto virtue I add knowledge, to knowledge I receive self-control and perseverance and godliness in the name of Jesus. These qualities are inherent and they grow in me continually in Jesus name. I increase in my knowledge of You. Grace is being multiplied unto me in the name of Jesus. Thank You for answered prayers.

CHAPTER TWO

Don't Go Larissa

We worked as a team; or at least, so it appeared. As if we were all connected as workers in the same organization or somehow connected to the same source.
The seven of us lived in the same house, left for work about the same time and we shared a common house keeper as well.

You see, this house keeper of ours was indispensable, a truly gentle soul, meek, faithful, committed and always

available to us all. She was there for everyone and yet personally connected to each individual.
A season came that I became so weary of work and started sleeping extra hours. Instead of regaining lost strength after the rest, the tiredness increased and I slept a little longer each time. Like a little more sleep led to even deeper slumber.

*"**A little sleep, a little slumber, a little folding of the hands to sleep. So shall your poverty come on you like a prowler**, And your need like an armed man." (Proverbs 6 verse 10-11 NKJV) Emphasis mine*

As if in a movie, I saw myself drift into further sleep, I could almost feel my tiredness and hear my deep snoring.
I heard and saw myself.
I was actually sleeping in a sleep.
And gentle Larrisa, our house keeper would wake me up every morning. On each occasion, I would rebuke her for waking me. I would sleep from when others went out to work till when they returned. This tiredness just never left me. And I slept more and more all the time.
This went on for times and days without end.

One particular morning, I heard one of my housemates discussing with Larrisa on the event of the previous day. In her gentle and quiet manner, she gave him counsel.

"Jude, for better results, simply take a break after each effort. Log into the database and then re-launch again. You will achieve much more than rushing it all at once. Always feel free to give me a call, that is what I'm here for."

She gave suggestions to him on how to achieve much more, lessons on effectiveness.

Larrisa is just too intelligent or so I thought within me.

Such a good and patient teacher

She wished him the best of the day and he left.

And so did other housemates; one after the other they all left.

She then came over to where I was sleeping, snoring away.

"Wake up Temi, it's time to start the day."

"You need to go conquer the day."

"Please go out and work."

And in anger, I warned her seriously never to wake me again.

I complained of tiredness and achy bones.

What I needed from her was empathy, not disturbance

With my voice raised, she receded, head bowed

She was out rightly sorrowful

Whether at my raised voice or at my slothfulness, I cannot tell

But the next day, it was different

As others went out to work, she came near me again

This conversation ensued between us.

"Temi, good morning."

"I am not here to disturb your sleep anymore"
"I just ask that you pay me my wages and relieve me of my duties"
"I am of no use to you, I need to go to where I'm needed."
"Get me my bag, let me pay you off!" I retorted
And as she left to bring my bag, it occurred to me that I would miss her
She was the gentlest soul I ever met
It also dawned on me that she handled every aspect of my life, my home front, my everything
There was virtually nothing I could do without her
Like a life support she was to me.
My very backbone
Ever since she came into my home, she took over all of my affairs
She updated me on all happenstances
She explained many things I didn't understand to me
Her gentle words had a way of penetrating into the very fibre of my being!
She made life so much easier for me
I could depend on her for help in any and every aspect of my life.
My personal assistant and yet in a humble way my boss
I would miss her
Would I ever find a replacement like her?
So faithful and patient
Vast in all affairs?
She knew and updated me about everything I needed to know

A true helper
And I imagined, something was about to be taken from me
Something tangible
Something real
Something indispensable
This something is a Someone!
Someone I couldn't live without
The Holy Spirit!
With a loud scream, I sharply jolted up from sleep
"Nooo! Don't leave me, nooo, don't go!"
"Larissa, please, I can't live without you"
"I mean; I need you"
"You came into my life and turned things around"
"My life, my home, my world would be in chaos without you"
"I can't imagine running my affairs without you"
"I can't live without you"
"Please!!!"
Alas! It was all a dream.

A dream like no other
Too real
Void of words to express the feeling.
I screamed so hard and so loud into reality that my husband sleeping next to me jolted from sleep too; asking what the matter was.
I recounted the experience to him
Trembling, sobbing

I was visibly shaken to every fibre of my being
Wishing I hadn't experienced such.
His counsel on that day was to go before the Lord and find where I had missed it. It was clearly a case of losing fervency and becoming slothful in God's service.
And we prayed.
That experience was just too deep for me.
In the course of the day, I meditated over that dream severally
My heart was sorrowful
Appetite flew out of the window all day
I kept asking for mercy
As if the ears of the Lord were heavy
"Lord! A broken and a contrite spirit surely you won't despise." Was my cry all day
I just wasn't myself
Like David, in Psalm 42 verse 3, tears became my food

*"**My tears have been my food day and night**, while they continually say to me, "Where is your God?" (Psalm 42 verse 3 NKJV) Emphasis mine*

Oh! How I missed it
How I slipped
And slumber took over.
I must have disappointed heaven
That Wednesday was a day of sober reflection for me.
I sobbed and wept before the Lord all day
That was a serious warning

I had been sleeping spiritually and the Lord was gracious enough to reach out to me in that dream explaining my spiritual state.
In the course of that day, I began to reflect on my life since I left the shores of Nigeria and moved to Aberdeen, Scotland with my family.
I began to recount the Lord's dealings with me and instructions He had given me before leaving the shores of my home country.
I had deviated from paying attention to His instructions.

Though we attended a living church in Aberdeen, I was operating below capacity. Many other affairs of life had taken over such that true communion and ministry efforts suffered. I contented myself with church attendance and involvement only when convenient.

The core things He called me to do were neglected.
It was summer of the year 2007. Even though I had confessed before the Lord, I still shared my dream with my prayer partner. The experience just wouldn't go away.

I was on the phone to her; a dear sister and friend, and as we spoke, she noticed the tone of my voice.
"Anything the matter?"
"Are you okay?"
"This is not the you I know."
I divulged all to her, shedding tears.

As I narrated to her, the reality of that experience came afresh.
I have always belonged to the school of those who open up on all matters; scripture admonishes us to confess our faults one to another and to never hide any sin if I want to overcome it.

Never would I cover any sin, I would rather share my faults with someone that can pray with me, so that deliverance can come in that area.
In doing so I have always received help from above.

As I divulged to her, I wept bitterly
"Please pray for me", I cried
"Please tell Him not to take His Holy Spirit from me"
"I can't survive without the Holy Spirit, please"
I wept bitterly
Still sobbing, I begged her to come over and help me out; and she came.
We prayed together and the heavens gave rain. Times of refreshing did come from His presence.
And as we prayed that day, the Spirit of the Lord reminded me of an occurrence; years back in my university days. It was almost a similar warning but this time from His words.

After giving my life to Christ at the university, a particular year came that I didn't perform well academically and I decided to reduce fellowship activities. After all, I was in the university to study so, serving God was secondary. Before I knew it, my prayer life dwindled, I started to grow cold.

One Saturday morning, I prayed earnestly and asked the Holy Spirit why things weren't the same in my prayer life, and why I was now struggling.
I just wasn't enjoying that fellowship and adventure in this Christian walk anymore, that sweet communion was missing.
I didn't have to wait long
A word flashed through my heart
Sharply.
I received a scripture. I quickly grabbed my Bible and opened to the scripture that flashed through my heart: Revelations 3 verse 15-16

"I know your works, that you are neither cold nor hot. I could wish you were cold or hot. So then, because you are lukewarm, and neither cold nor hot, I will vomit you out of My mouth" (Revelations 3 verse 15-16, NKJV)

I exclaimed!
"Lord my academic performance wasn't so good last semester and I want to give my academics priority. Don't I deserve some words of comfort at least?"
And I had wept then too.

I recall I had also shared with a dear friend then and we prayed together asking for forgiveness and that the Lord would restore me to fellowship.
This was a second warning; first in 1994 and then 2007.
One thing I had learnt early and quickly in my Christian walk is to maximize the scripture in James 5 verse 16

*"**Confess your trespasses to one another, and pray for one another, that you may be healed.** The effective, fervent prayer of a righteous man avails much." (James 5 verse 16) Emphasis mine*

Hear me beloved, God takes our relationship with Him serious and expects the same from us. It is worth mentioning at this point that my poor academic performance the previous semester was not a case of over zealousness in serving God but that of misplaced priority and poor planning plus poor time management. I needed to apply discipline to the management of my time overall. In the latter case of Aberdeen, I simply had my priorities misplaced.

The relocation had enough changes it offered. I was just too busy pursuing my career while my spiritual life suffered. It was a true state of spiritual slumber compared to where I was coming from.

"Never be lacking in zeal, but keep your spiritual fervour, serving the Lord." (Romans 12 verse 11 NIV)

Let me digress at this point to say when we perform below capacity, it is a subtle form of backsliding because to whom much is given, much is expected

"But he who did not know, yet committed things deserving of stripes, shall be beaten with few. ***For everyone to whom much is given, from him much will be required; and to whom much has been committed, of him they will ask the more." (Luke 12 verse 48 NKJV)*** *Emphasis mine*

It is a terrible thing to live without the presence of the Holy Spirit. Such experience is best left to the imagination. 1 Samuel 28: 3-25 gives an interesting account; when the Spirit of the Lord departed from Saul, it became an issue for him to hear from God or to receive directions. The frustration of not hearing for one who had enjoyed divine guidance led him to consulting a medium out of desperation. He consulted with a witch at En Dor

"And when Saul inquired of the Lord, the Lord did not answer him, either by dreams or by Urim or by the prophets. Then Saul said to his servants, "Find me a woman who is a medium, that I may go to her and inquire of her." And his servants said to him, "In fact, there is a woman who is a medium at En Dor." (1 Samuel 28 verse 6-7, NKJV)

Having enjoyed counsel, leading, help, teachings and even convictions by the Holy Spirit, it would be a miserable life to exist one day without His indwelling. The comfort however is that God would always call those He loves to order. He could issue a warning and in some cases, mete with discipline.

When the Lord spoke to me during my university days from Revelations 3:15-16, God was referring to deeds. Two things God frowns at in the lives of His children are sin and spiritual slothfulness. Therefore, the above mentioned scripture should actually motivate and comfort a true child of God.
Why? Or how? You may be asking.

A picture that readily comes to mind was an occasion when my first son accompanied me to get groceries. He was four or five years old if I remember correctly; he wanted candy, then he pointed at a box of cookies and later chocolates. He threw tantrums as I insisted he would have none because we had some of those items back at home. As an African mother, I gave him the necessary "healing" as cure from such indiscipline when we got home. Never did he or his sister point at any item on any shopping visit thereafter. On subsequent visits to stores, people had commented on how well behaved they are. If only they knew the "healing" sessions that had been done behind the scene!

I had watched a similar scenario whereby a boy screamed and rolled on the floor when his mom refused him ice cream. I dare not step into the situation to correct such a child as I would do to my own child; best left to the mom to handle the situation her own way. So much so, the Lord would only discipline those that are His. He has no business rebuking anyone not fully yielded to His will.

So, I see it as a great privilege to be counted worthy of His rebuke. While He is working on us to conform us to His glorious image, any disparity in our lives will not go unchecked by Him.

"Now no chastening seems to be joyful for the present, but painful; nevertheless, afterward it yields the peaceable fruit of righteousness to those who have been trained by it." (Hebrews 12 verse 11, NKJV)

He disciplines us for our good because rebuke, correction and love are all part of the package.

"As many as I love, I rebuke and chasten. Therefore, be zealous and repent." (Revelations 3 verse 19, NKJV)

Hot and cold as described by Jesus in Rev 3 verse 15 are useful and good but lukewarmness is what Jesus frowns at.

"I know your works, that you are neither cold nor hot. I could wish you were cold or hot. So then, because you are lukewarm,

and neither cold nor hot, I will vomit you out of My mouth." (Revelation 3:15-16 NKJV)

Lukewarmness depicts spiritual sloppiness or slothfulness in terms of service to the Lord. Being spat out of the mouth was a rebuke. Gospel truth is, our God is a loving Father that is plenteous in mercy. Having taken time to invest so much in us, He wouldn't want to just throw us out hence He corrects, prunes and chastises His own beloved.

A deeper insight on Revelation 3:15-16 gave illustration of Laodecea, a city located between Heiropolis and Colossae; these two cities surrounding Laodecea were known for possession of pure waters flowing through them. Heiropolis had a spring flowing with hot, medicinal water while Colossae had cold refreshing mountain springs. Laodecea had dirty lukewarm water. By the time the water from Heirpolis flowed to Laodecea, the hotness had gone out as there were no heating system as we have today.

The Lukewarm water in Laodecea when and if tasted by visitors is almost spat out immediately after tasting. This water was never fresh; neither was it hot or cold. The concept of water being lukewarm wasn't new to Laodecea and so Christ was making a point to the Christians there using an illustration they could relate with, their daily reality. Their lukewarm water

presented a problem, it was useless. It was not useful for a refreshing drink neither was it hot enough to be therapeutic.
As I prepared the manuscript of this story, autumn was fast giving way to winter and the temperature drop was much more felt. To this the kettle boiled more often for tea, chocolate drink and when occasion demands, coffee. I had this very day made a cup of tea which I kept by my side as I typed away on my laptop. When I raised my head about half an hour later, reached for the mug and took a sip, I simply spewed it back, threw the content away and made a fresh one. For me, it just has to be hot.

Again the impact of a cold drink in a hot sunny day is best left imagined.

*"**As cold water to a weary soul**, so is good news from a far country." (Proverbs 25 verse 25) Emphasis mine*

And I could picture my heavenly father!
Question to you and I is this: "Would Jesus use the word, lukewarm in describing you and I today?"

Shall we pray?

1. Father, I approach Your presence with a heart of thanksgiving this hour. (Psalm 100 verse 4-5). Thank You for Your Word which is never scarce in my generation. Thank You for rebukes, thank You for chastisement. You

correct those You love and I am privileged to be one of them (Revelation 3:19). I am so thankful for Your love for me. Thank You for another opportunity to get it right. Truly, I`m grateful. Receive my thanksgiving in Jesus name.

2. Humbly, I come before You today realising that You despise lukewarmness. Your Word says if I regard iniquity in my heart You will not hear me (Psalm 66 verse 8), therefore I confess every act of lukewarmness in the spirit. I ask that You forgive me in any way that I have performed less than the expectation of heaven over my life. I pray that You forgive every inconsistency in my walk with You. Wherever I have misplaced priorities or not given You Your rightful place in my life, have mercy. Do not cast me away from Your presence I pray (Psalm 51 verse 11)

3. Father, keep me alert, keep me awake spiritually. I will not be a victim of any spiritual slumber, slothfulness or sloppiness in Jesus. Lukewarmness is far from me in Jesus name. Henceforth, I will not misplace priorities. The love for fame, career, wealth, ambition, sin and self will not overshadow my communion with you. By Your power, nothing will take me away from Your presence. Zechariah 4 verse 6a says: "It is not by power, by might but by my spirit"

4. Holy Spirit, please don't stop Your gracious dealings in my life. I give You full permission to lead me on. Give me more of Your presence. You are my Senior Partner, pour afresh upon me the spirit of grace and supplication (Zechariah 12 verse 10)

5. Dear Holy Spirit, You were the Spirit present at creation, I ask You today, please brood over my life and cause illumination to come in every aspect. I desire Your light to shine in every aspect of my life. I subject my life to Your scrutiny. By my spirit man, reveal issues I need to resolve in my inward man (Proverbs 20 verse 27)

6. In any aspect where I have slacked or lagged behind, give me speed, grant me strength to catch up. Let divine speed be granted to me so I can run and burn for You. Let Your holy fire burn off every sloppiness in my life. I will not grieve or bring You sorrow by my actions. I will yield to Your promptings always as You bid me in Jesus' name.

7. Lord in times of weariness or discouragement, plant helpers around me, give me friends that will sharpen me (Proverbs 27 verse 17). Give me covenant friends that will challenge and encourage me in my walk with You. I refuse to walk this journey alone, make help available for me always in Jesus name.

8. Father, I am grateful because You heard me. Unto You that answers prayers shall all flesh come. You do not store prayers, You answer prayers. Therefore, I am persuaded that every supplication receives Your attention today in the name of Jesus (Psalm 65 verse 2).

CHAPTER THREE

The Fifth Request

As I held the microphone again to speak, this dog showed up as usual.

For whatever activity I was involved in, that dog was always near.

That same black dog

It was here again licking my leg.

It had licked my right leg continually, a particular spot on my right ankle.

It followed me wherever I went.

Always present whenever I had something to achieve

Like we had signed a pact together

But I never liked dogs

My dislike for dogs dated way back to my childhood days; round about when I was nine years old. My parents both worked in Ibadan, Oyo State, South Western part of Nigeria. We lived in an estate at the suburbs. There were many houses in that estate, or call it a condominium, it was a mixed community of many nationalities; Africans, Europeans, Latinos and Asians.

On this day after school, I headed for one of the houses in the estate in company of three other friends who lived in the neighbourhood. We were headed for that house because it had an almond tree. We wanted to pluck almond fruits. It was almond season and this tree in the house offered the best. I had passed there two days ago and observed they were ripening up.

Typically, I did the tree climbing, Tolu, my next door neighbour passed the long stick while Tamara and Nike picked the fruits in a plastic bag we brought along.
From nowhere, this German shepherd dog came barking. We had never seen it before. Everyone scattered and ran. I was stuck on the tree.

With everyone out of sight and the dog barking at me, I decided to come down and hit the dog with my long stick. That should scare it off while I made my escape or so I thought.

Unfortunately, my stick broke as I landed, a part of me wanted to stay put but I ran out of confusion and then got bitten by this dog. It literarily charged at my left thigh, tore through my dress and I felt the pain from the bite.

As I managed to get home, I was in tears, not from the pain of the bite but from the shock and outturn of that late afternoon event. It had never happened before. We had always been free as kids to move freely within that community.

My parents were not back from work and I dared not mention the incident to my father. I however confided in my siblings' nanny. She immediately suggested we talk with the cook, Uncle James we called him.

As I narrated all to him, he advised we head for the clinic.
"Temi, if we don't go to the clinic today and get you vaccinated, you will start barking like a dog from 5am tomorrow morning. A lot of dogs have rabies." He said
At this I panicked.
I nearly passed out at the thought of waking from my bed the next morning and instead of talking, I would be barking like a dog.
"You mean the dog's voice will come out of my mouth when I try to talk? So, is it like a snake bite that injects poison into someone?"

"Daddy will get to know if I go to the clinic."
"Yes, like a dog and I mean that. Better for your dad to know, Temi. You don't want to wake up tomorrow morning barking like a dog, do you?" Reluctantly, I obliged.

My father, after reprimanding me eventually investigated the owner of the dog. What exactly ensued between them I do not know but that incident marked my abhorrence for dogs.
It so turned out I didn't need any vaccine as the dog was well immunized

Back to my story.
I was busy and couldn't entertain anything that would take my focus away from those activities. But this dog kept licking my right ankle. Initially, my attitude was to ignore hoping it would go away but I noticed it kept coming after me and had such boldness to get so close to me. Its effrontery was a cause for worry.

Definitely, there was more than meets the eye and this had to be dealt with. Something must be an attraction to this persistent animal.
Such annoying distraction!

I shifted my gaze from what I was doing; angrily but firmly, I addressed the dog asking it to back off. Instead of backing off, it continued wagging its tail and licking

my leg. What was the attraction? As I tried shaking my leg off and to simultaneously kick at it, it kept coming back, focused on that spot on my leg and wagging its tail. More like the dog was saying to me "I have a stake here!"
And thereafter, I woke up.
It was all a dream.
So vivid, so real.
And I meditated and tried to make sense of the whole encounter.

I had the same dream a few days later.
Repeated
Rehashed
Replicated
Just that this time, it went further from where I woke up the last time;
The same repeated scenes
But as I tried to kick the dog away this time,
I heard a voice challenging me.
So I turned to the direction of that voice and saw the owner of the dog. I could just tell they were connected. He was a very dark young man clothed in black confronting me with such anger and defending the dog. I stood helpless, powerless, speechless, just stunned as I took it all in.

I knew the Lord was calling my attention to something. The message was clear, precise, concise, sharp and exact. There was an exposure.

A leak somewhere
A hedge had been broken.
Why else should I be so helpless as that guy hurled insult at me?
And he did it sarcastically.
Such grave Insult
Defamatory and degrading words
Highly derogatory remarks
And with such boldness
To say the least, not complimentary
I could read hatred in his eyes.
And not even a scripture came from me to counter attack!
Self-defensive words eluded me!

As I meditated all day on that occurrence, sound counsel and knowledge from comparing scripture with scriptures revealed I had a "wound" which had not been healed that was a great attraction to the dog.

Remember Lazarus whose sores were licked by dogs? (Luke 16 verse 21)

"desiring to be fed with the crumbs which fell from the rich man's table. ***Moreover, the dogs came and licked his sores."*** *(Luke 16 verse 21 NKJV) Emphasis mine*

For sores naturally attract dogs or at least flies.
Well, what caused sores or wounds in my own case?

I had been hurt by certain people and had resolved to keep away from such persons rather than opening up to God to heal me of such hurts.

Summarily, I was unknowingly harbouring un-forgiveness. Sometimes, we close up on people in our hearts after we are offended but play cool and matured about it. We believe avoiding those people or keeping them at arm's length is the solution. And then, before we know it, we begin to resent such people in our hearts.

Though the wounds were not open, it was still fresh enough "spiritually" to attract dogs in my own case. At every attempt that I kept trying to do God's work, I was always distracted, ineffective. More like a blunt knife which couldn't cut effectively, so much effort would be required to achieve little impact. I needed to remove the dross from the silver in order to be effective again.

"Take away the dross from silver. And it will go to the silversmith for jewellery." (Proverbs 25 verse 4 NKJV)

I had given the devil a foothold. An unresolved issue or un-forgiveness captures the soul which hinders us from living fully for God or serving Him with all our heart. It dulls our spiritual senses

Friends, un-forgiveness is worse than adultery, it eats one up, and renders one incapacitated. Jesus was able to declare boldly to his disciples that the devil could not lay hold of anything with which to accuse Him before God. May the devil not find anything in us (John 14 verse 30)

"I will no longer talk much with you, ***for the ruler of this world is coming, and he has nothing in Me"*** *(John 14 verse 30 NKJV) Emphasis mine*

The dark guy in my dream stood as my accuser. Like he had a legal right and he was right! I had broken a spiritual law and given the devil a foothold. Despite the mercy and forgiveness of God that is available, the law enforcer is the devil and his demons and they stand before God accusing us day and night. God is often "helpless" as He cannot break His own principles.

With that heart of un-forgiveness, the devil sees and capitalizes on that to accuse us before God

"Then I heard a loud voice saying in heaven, "Now salvation, and strength, and the kingdom of our God, and the power of His Christ have come, ***for the accuser of our brethren, who accused them before our God day and night****, has been cast down." (Rev 12:10 NKJV) Emphasis mine*

"Then he showed me Joshua the high priest standing before the Angel of the Lord, and ***Satan standing at his right hand to oppose him****." (Zechariah 3:1 NKJV) Emphasis mine*

Despite Joshua being a high priest, the devil still withstood him before God!

As believers, we must consciously and consistently make the effort to resist the devil and give him no foothold to stand upon in our lives. Many offenses are actually baits the devil uses to get us. Most times we have logical reasons to hold on to such offenses, however, the Spirit of the Lord says to let it go. It does more harm to you the offended than the offender.

"Lest Satan should take advantage of us; for we are not ignorant of his devices." (2 Corinthians 2:11 NKJV)

In my situation, I simply prayed asking for grace to correct all wrongs and amazingly, His gracious dealings started two days after I prayed. The experience that followed herein further confirmed the interpretation from the encounter in the two reoccurring dreams.

My car had been scheduled for the annual MOT tests at a city 55 minutes away from where I resided. It was not uncommon for booking in my city to be so filled with no possibility of getting an appointment before the impounding officers take to the street. So I booked in the very next city to Macae where I lived then. I had set out early that morning and arrived at the venue on time. The whole exercise went well that beautiful Tuesday morning and in no distant time, I was heading back to Macae city.

As I drove back from the city called Casimiro de Abreu, alone in the car, I had this visitation. While singing to a worship song from the CD playing in the car, I suddenly felt His presence.
Then I felt this "thing" in my heart
A contrite feeling
It was like an arrow pierced through my heart, I was heavy! The Holy Spirit laid upon my heart three people I needed to reconcile with and forgive urgently.
They flashed so quickly through my mind's eye.
I tell you my heart was be-laboured. It was like the hurt was fully reopened, like the opening of a covered wound and I was bleeding in my heart. But it was an answer to the prayers prayed two days earlier.

You see, they had really hurt me and I felt I had a right to lock them out.
In retrospect, I actually locked them in.
Two of these people were easily within reach so I reached out with an olive branch. I was then left with making a long distant call to the third person.

The Lord helped me. It was like grace was released for that purpose. You see, handling the first two was easy though it caused me humbling myself and surrendering my self-will to the Lord. The third wasn't so easy as the person in question was much elderly and had a sense of entitlement. As a matter of fact, I hurt more from making that third contact but I just had to depend on the Holy Spirit's help and console myself with the fact that I obeyed his leading.

I came to the conclusion that depending on the circumstance, it might be advisable to sit and talk things over. It would ensure no wounds are covered without fully healing up. We must however bear in mind that not all people are agreeable when approached.

My encounter with the third person in question made me understand better what Apostle Paul meant when he said in 2 Thessalonians 3 verse 2, "not all men had faith". There are many, even of those who have received a measure of the divine light, in whom we cannot trust; they are irregular, disorderly, and cannot be brought under regular discipline. Faith in this sense isn't about believing God, some are just difficult to relate with.

"And that we may be delivered from unreasonable and wicked men for not all have faith" (2 Thessalonians 3 verse 2 NKJV)

Gospel truth is, often times, you just need to forgive in your heart without having to meet for discussion with such people, after all, Jesus never visited any Pharisee. He just chose to forgive them for they knew not what they did. It's a thing of the heart. Stephen also had developed a heart of forgiving even before offenses were committed.

"Then he knelt down and cried out with a loud voice, "Lord, do not charge them with this sin." *And when he had said this, he fell asleep. (Acts 7 verse 60 NKJV.) Emphasis mine*

With a predetermined mind set, we can choose to forgive ahead even before the offense is committed.
Recounting the Lord's prayer in Matthew 6: 9-13, the **Fifth Request** was the only request with a condition: asking the Lord to forgive us our sins as we do same to those who offend us.

"In this manner, therefore, pray: Our Father in heaven, Hallowed be Your name. Your kingdom come. Your will be done on earth as it is in heaven. Give us this day our daily bread. ***And forgive us our debts, as we forgive our debtors.*** *And do not lead us into temptation, but deliver us from the evil one. For Yours is the kingdom and the power and the glory forever. Amen." (Matthew 6 verse 9-13 NKJV) Emphasis mine*

Though we have been taught so much about the love of God and God's forgiving acts; we need to emphasize forgiving others as a prerequisite. Many of us just recite the Lord's prayer without paying attention to the significance of this condition **'as we forgive those who**

trespass against us'. We must be careful to pay attention to such words lest they just become religious prayers.

Why do we find it so hard to let go?
Why do we feel a sense of joy when people who have offended us suffer some misfortune?
Can there be some form of pleasure we derive in not forgiving others?
It must be that un-forgiveness gives some form of pleasure otherwise we won't hold on to things if they hurt.

Ever tried asking God to forgive you to the very extent to which you forgive others?
Shall we make up our minds to forgive quickly?
In so doing, we release people immediately.
Shall we make excuses for people when they offend us; even before the offense is committed?
It is possible to reason that such people are only operating based on their level of understanding. They could also have lashed out based on what they were going through. So, don't hold on to, or ignore that grudge in your heart. That friend, that boss, that colleague, that in-law, that neighbour, that spouse; whatever it is they have done to you, let it go! ***For they know not what they do!***

*"Then Jesus said, "**Father, forgive them, for they do not know what they do.**" And they divided His garments and cast lots" (Luke 23 verse 34 NKJV) Emphasis mine*

It is pertinent that we never ignore grudges in our heart; instead, deal with them immediately! Let's ask the Lord to dissolve in us that critical and judgmental spirit.

Please permit me to share four reminders from Matthew chapter 18; based on the parable of the unforgiving servant

"Then Peter came to Him and said, "Lord, how often shall my brother sin against me, and I forgive him? Up to seven times?" Jesus said to him, "I do not say to you, up to seven times, but up to seventy times seven. Therefore, the kingdom of heaven is like a certain king who wanted to settle accounts with his servants. And when he had begun to settle accounts, one was brought to him who owed him ten thousand talents. But as he was not able to pay, his master commanded that he be sold, with his wife and children and all that he had, and that payment be made. The servant therefore fell down before him, saying, 'Master, have patience with me, and I will pay you all.' Then the master of that servant was moved with compassion, released him, and forgave him the debt. "But that servant went out and found one of his fellow servants who owed him a hundred denarii; and he laid hands on him and took him by the throat, saying, 'Pay me what you owe!' So his fellow servant fell down at his feet and begged him, saying, 'Have patience

with me, and I will pay you all.' And he would not, but went and threw him into prison till he should pay the debt. So when his fellow servants saw what had been done, they were very grieved, and came and told their master all that had been done. Then his master, after he had called him, said to him, 'You wicked servant! I forgave you all that debt because you begged me. Should you not also have had compassion on your fellow servant, just as I had pity on you?' And his master was angry, and delivered him to the torturers until he should pay all that was due to him. "So My Heavenly Father also will do to you if each of you, from his heart, does not forgive his brother his trespasses," (Matthew 18 verse 27-35 NKJV) Emphasis mine

1) Un-forgiveness can lead to the reinstatement of debts initially written off.
"And his master was angry, and delivered him to the torturers ***until he should pay all that was due to him."*** *(Verse 34) Emphasis mine*

2) God calls a man who does not forgive a wicked man because un-forgiveness is a deliberate choice. But Jesus said the merciful shall obtain mercy; conversely, the unmerciful cannot obtain mercy.
"Then his master, after he had called him, said to him, 'You wicked servant! I forgave you all that debt because you begged me. Should you not also have had compassion on your fellow servant, just as I had pity on you?' (Verses 32-33)

3) God gets angry with such a man

*"**And his master was angry,** and delivered him to the torturers until he should pay all that was due to him. (Verse 34) Emphasis mine*

4) It can open doors to demonic attacks or sicknesses.
"And his master was angry, and ***delivered him to the torturers*** *until he should pay all that was due to him. (Verse 34) Emphasis mine*

Spiritual gifts, knowledge and more understanding of the truth is good, however, what makes for spiritual maturity is denial of self-will. Or better put, ability to surrender my will for God's will - that ability to yield to Him.

I may not be able to control my memory and forget the hurt or harm done to me but I can control my will and choose God's laid down path of forgiveness. By this we are being warned and in keeping them, there's great reward (Psalm 19 verse 11).

"Moreover by them Your servant is warned, and in keeping them there is great reward" (Psalm 19 verse 11 NKJV)

You hard heartedness leading to un-forgiveness, the Lord rebuke you! Un-forgiveness must go lest it poisons that glorious future the Lord has for you. I learnt in no small measure from that experience the importance of unburdening myself of any weight, baggage or whatever can keep me down. Whatever stands as a weight holds me down spiritually and must be avoided by all means.

"Therefore we also, since we are surrounded by so great a cloud of witnesses, ***let us lay aside every weight, and the sin which so easily ensnares us,*** *and let us run with endurance the race that is set before us" (Hebrews 12 verse 1 NKJV) (Verse 34) Emphasis mine*

After I released and reconciled with those three people from and in my heart, I experienced tremendous joy! Oh what joy, what peace, what release but above all, what boldness! Beloved, grace is available this hour. Be ready for Christ's coming – Let's forgive everyone.

Shall we pray?

1. Father, I am very grateful for Your gracious dealings in my life. I celebrate Your being mindful of me always. Thank You for always revealing where the devil has a stronghold in my life. Thank You for exposing and frustrating His plans. All glory to Your holy name.

2. Lord, for every act of un-forgiveness, high and hard heartedness, I ask for mercy today. For taking Your word with levity, I plead for Your mercy. I have been disobedient to Your word and allowed my feelings to rule, please forgive me. I have not submitted fully to Your precepts, please be merciful. Truly, forgiveness

resides with You that we may fear You (Psalm 130:4). Wash and cleanse me by the blood in Jesus' name

3. Jesus, as You reveal secrets and matters of my life to me, I receive quick understanding and grace to make amends. I receive knowledge from above on how to make peace, I receive insight on how to handle issues. I receive wisdom on relating with all men. I make peace with all men, I let go of offenses, I love sincerely, I forgive quickly, I bear no grudge in Jesus' name.

4. Every hedge that I have broken ignorantly, let the blood of Jesus avail for me. For every exposure, please cover and defend me. You spoke for Joshua the high priest before the accuser; Lord by Your mercy, speak for me and defend my lot. Let every filthy garment be taken off me today in Jesus' name.

5. Every accuser of my life, the Lord silences You! The blood of Jesus is against You. Every voice of accusation against my life; and every tongue rising in judgement against me, I condemn. Your voice holds no water; it carries no weight in Jesus' name. Your counsel against me is turned to foolishness. Every arrow of words hurled at me is rendered useless in Jesus' name.

6. Lord, today, I receive healing from every hurt, offense, bitterness and all forms of un-forgiveness. Help me to totally let go. Help me to mean it from my heart. I

will resolve issues quickly based on Your laid down precepts and not on my own judgement. I receive marvellous help, let Your grace be sufficient for me. Give me a deeper understanding on this matter in Jesus name.

7. I receive grace to make amends where necessary, I choose to correct all wrongs. Grant me the needed grace to humble myself. Let me yield to Your leading always. I silence every voice of self, every voice of logic raging within me. Let Your Word and Your voice rule in my heart

8. Father, henceforth, no torment of hell is strong enough to hold me down. Every torment in any aspect of my life ends today. As I follow Your precepts, let the reward of obedience follow me. I surrender my will for Yours. I receive by impartation the ability to yield always in Jesus name.

CHAPTER FOUR

An Arabian Prince

"Sure, sounds okay. Quite appealing, I must confess."

"Can I request for the P&L and other related documents by email?" I asked.

And there was silence, more of a distraction at the other end.

Then she replied;

"Yes Ma`am! I will have them forwarded to your inbox in no time. Emm, could you please confirm your email address again?" Came the response.

I gave email details, and I quickly requested for time to familiarize myself with all the documents and then I added.

"Once I'm on top of it, I will be in touch, thanks very much and enjoy the rest of your day."
"Thanks Mrs F, and if you need any further clarifications too, please don't hesitate to make contact."

Just as we hung up, I heard email beeps; three of them actually and as I flipped through, I realized it was from the same source – the lady I just spoke with.
A prospective business partner.
My initial reaction was "Wow! They sure mean business; didn't even allow me blink an eye."
I never knew the lady before but someone had connected us together as we both had something to offer in collaboration.
Opportunity on a platter of gold.
I couldn't place my finger on it but for some reason, I was just unnecessarily slow about progressing on this matter.
Cautious
Circumspect
Leery or shall I say wary?
And the days rolled by.

I received reminders requesting for update; they were waiting for my decision. All I kept doing was asking for more time. I must be sure before giving any answer.
So I searched for that certainty and conviction.
Just to be sure God was involved in this.

During one of my discussions on this subject with my husband, he simply said, "Well, all I can say is, they won't wait forever so you need to make up your mind soon."
That sent me thinking on the urge to take out time to pray and pray through on this matter.
I became much more determined to find out what God had to say on this matter. Like David, I went the "inquiry prayer" way.

Again this lady called and as we spoke, she asked if anything was the matter and that she was available to answer all my questions.
So I spilled it out, I came out straight and said,
"Well, Mrs G, you are a Christian and you know how these things work. I was just waiting for that green light within me to be sure God is in this."
Then I left the rest hanging
She said she understood and inquired to know how much longer she should wait.
"As soon as I have the go ahead, I will call." Was my response.

And then I started to weigh her last statement: asking me how much longer to wait was like asking me when God would speak. Hasn't she read that he that believes makes no haste?

"Therefore thus says the Lord God: "Behold, I lay in Zion a stone for a foundation, a tried stone, a precious cornerstone, a sure foundation; ***Whoever believes will not act hastily."*** *(Isaiah 28:16 NKJV) Emphasis mine*

You see, I had burnt my fingers on two occasions and had learnt the importance of waiting on God to be sure He was involved. I refuse bowing to any pressure irrespective of whom or where it was coming from. It's all beyond logic.

You see, many years ago, a business had gone way overboard; and so I cried to God with tears asking where I had gone wrong. I challenged Him concerning His promise of profit for all my labour as well as prospering me in whatsoever I do.
The only response was the Holy Spirit reminding me of Proverbs 3:5-6 saying I handled things my own way and should always acknowledge Him for all at every stage instead of expecting Him to fit into my business plans.

"Trust in the Lord with all your heart, and lean not on your own understanding; In all your ways acknowledge Him, And He shall direct your paths." (Proverbs 3:5-6 NKJV)

At that time, I had sincerely acted confidently based on my past experience and made logical conclusions that one plus one should naturally equate to two.

God really wants to be Lord over all our affairs. He wants to be involved in all that pertains to us. You can't shut Him out of one department while you open some other departments to Him. He must be Lord of all. I mean if you are interested in that intimate walk and wish to go all the way with Him.

In the Book of Leviticus, the Lord went as far as telling the children of Israel what to eat, what to wear, what to think, how to act, where to go, how to behave and even as far as giving them laws of hygiene. God was interested in every aspect of their lives just as He is in ours today.

Someone may be asking; "why then did God give us brains? Well, I need not ask God if I need to eat or take a bath. Yes, there is a place for ***common sense*** in all we do but it's best to go with the ***higher sense*** when delicate issues are involved.

Well, it was obvious no response was forthcoming to my prayers. So I continued to maintain my watch to hear what He would say on the matter.

On one Tuesday, I promised giving my final response by the end of the week. So I settled down with God asking Him again what His counsel was on this matter. I told Him I had made a commitment to the lady for Friday. I reminded Him of His words and that since I follow Him,

I must have light on this matter and that I refuse to remain in the dark.

"Then Jesus spoke to them again, saying, "I am the light of the world. He who follows Me shall not walk in darkness, but have the light of life." (John 8:12 NKJV)

And so I prayed earnestly Tuesday, Wednesday, Thursday but nothing came. Sincerely, if dreams were birds that fly, I would have caught all as I was so alert for any and every signal. You could say my antennas were really up. At any and every opportunity, I was praying in the spirit. While I conversed with many, I was still listening within. I kept praying, "Lord, send a word, give me a vision, or a trance, or let it pop out from scriptures, speak to my hearing; I'm waiting for your voice. Holy Spirit, show me. Lord just do it Your way and minister to my heart".

And then dawn came that Friday, yet no response! About 6.00am that fateful morning, as I laid in bed, disappointed, wondering how to frame my words to the lady about my inability to proceed, I suddenly heard my phone beep.
It was an email.

I picked the phone and opened my email. It was from my prospective business partner; she sent a two-line email saying she had forgotten to attach this particular link and that she hoped it would further guide my decision before we speak later on in the day.

As I clicked on the link, I was taken to the company's website, for some reason, my eyes roved till a particular subsection flickered and as I opened that section, there laid the answer!
A discovery like no other.
An abhorrence!
Nothing but a snare of the devil
It was a no show for me; compromise against my faith stared at me.

The Amplified version of the Bible makes Apostle Paul's warning to his protégée, Timothy in 1Timothy 1 verse 19 clearer! He admonished Timothy to keep his faith and to have a good conscience; leaning completely on God with absolute trust and confidence in His guidance. Thank God, we have been exempted from the list of such who have rejected their moral compasses.

"keeping your faith [leaning completely on God with absolute trust and confidence in His guidance] and having a good conscience; for some [people] have rejected [their moral compass] and have made a shipwreck of their faith." (1Timothy 1verse 19, AMP)

At that moment I broke down in worship, thanking God for grace to wait upon Him for this long and for not acting by sight.
Gotta love John 8 verse 12!!!

". . . He who follows Me will not walk in the darkness . . ."

Mighty deliverer!!
He didn't tell me but He showed me.

*"Call to Me and I will answer you, and tell you [**and even show you**] great and mighty things, [things which have been confined and hidden], which you do not know and understand and cannot distinguish." (Jeremiah 33 verse 3 AMP)*
Emphasis mine

Sometimes God delays us by not showing up at our time but His timing is always perfect. He uses delay often to grow and mature our trust in Him, at other times, it may be to get our attention on certain issues.

Friends, money would have flooded in but not true riches; my conscience too would have gradually become seared as one thing would have led to another. The devil comes but for to kill, to steal and then finally destroy says John 10 verse 10.

*"**The thief does not come except to steal, and to kill, and to destroy**. I have come that they may have life, and that they*

may have it more abundantly" (John 10:10 NKJV) Emphasis mine

My conscience would have been killed gradually because the commitment to be made would make it difficult to back out or walk out on. Secondly, every divine deposit would have been stolen and thirdly, it would have taken only the mercy of God not to lose my salvation totally.

I went into these details; though without specifics, to let us know that the devil comes subtly and he knows areas in our lives to target. He is a bloody devourer; he is not your friend. He knew my yearnings at that season and had packaged things up properly to get me reeled in to his snare. In a very subtle manner too. You allow him come in through a key hole and he grows to occupy the whole house.

"Nor give any place to the devil" (Ephesians 4 verse 27 NKJV)

However, the Lord had taken time to teach me through those two painful experiences I had years back on the act of waiting on Him before taking any major decision.
I will like to share with you a revelation the Lord showed me before this business proposal came. The Spirit of God vividly brought it to my mind as I was rejoicing and thanking God for the mighty deliverance. And it all connected together.

About two months prior to the business proposal coming to me, I had this revelation.

I was in front of an Arabian Prince, he was tall, with beards covering both sides of the chin and had this sun tanned mulatto skin.

He was robed in a full Jellabiya attire; I cannot recollect clearly whether it was white or cream but it was a bright colour.

He had their usual ghutra on his head.

He reeked of wealth from head to toe.

An air of affluence

He kept staring at me, smiling, lustfully

He had that *"come, get me babe"* look in his eyes as I stared at him

And then a third personality was present with us

Well known to me

Nudging me to go ahead and marry the Arabian Prince

I was puzzled and couldn't make sense of it

"Temi, marrying this guy would solve all financial issues for life, you will be made, I tell you."

I considered those words and for a second; thought about the comfort.

Appealing, I dare say

But in a flash, I got my senses and will back.

Then I screamed:

"But am already married to someone else! Even if I wasn't, why would an uncircumcised Philistine be an attraction?" I was very angry at the person who tried convincing me, furious in my spirit and then I woke up.

I prayed earnestly asking God to deliver me from every wrong influence and grace never to compromise. I even prayed against falling into adultery!
I summarize what the Spirit of God spoke to my heart as I was thanking Him for that deliverance:

1. That business deal would have brought you wealth undoubtedly; but not riches from me.

2. The marriage to that Arabian Prince signified your business collaboration if you had gone into it, a partnership would have been formed.

3. The prince would have dictated the terms and since he was the husband, you would have had no choice but to dance to his whims. Compromise to your faith would have set in. Your faith would have become shipwrecked.

Please hear me: God's leading is **real** today as it was in the days of old. Not only in business but this applies to every facet of life.
Have you heard people say "We are praying on it?". Those are sayings of the wise and prudent, please follow their example. It doesn't matter how long you have to consistently tarry in the place of prayer, keep doing it, or better still, just **stay there!!!** No action till the leading comes. And if no leading comes, it means maintain status quo, **stay as you are**, don't take any action. It goes

beyond the physical sight judgment. What seems right may not be totally correct.

Yes! Let that opportunity go, the one He ordained for you will come.
Let that man go, the real one will wait for you.
Please allow them mock and scorn, they will still come back to celebrate His glory in your life.
Human opinions are temporary and subject to change. They may disapprove your principles but no one can doubt evidences and infallible proofs. Call it "the old fashioned way" but results always speak.

If per chance, you genuinely missed His leading in any area of life, your Heavenly Father knows how to compensate double for every pain. It is all about the sincerity of the heart.

Lord, please put a barricade between me and any so called "destiny helper" that will take me to Babylon. I pray for this reader, may that connection that will interfere with your prayer altar not see the light of day. I ask also that, may any prosperity that quenches spiritual fire remain afar off. May you not lose your salvation for temporary comfort and riches in Jesus's name.

I always feel saddened when a believer says things like "Ah, it's the reigning business, people are making money thereby...". In other words, they just flow with the wind. Without any vision and sense of purpose.

Friend, **check it out** first, don't rush into it. Never be in haste, again I say **check it out**. His leading guarantees peace when the storms blow, because it will always blow. If that applause has no approval from heaven, we'd rather close our eyes to it.

Is any presently in a tight corner due to actions taken without His leading? And it looks like the centre isn't holding anymore? There is hope. The book of Jeremiah promised when we seek Him with all our hearts we shall find Him. (Jeremiah 29 verse 13). As you earnestly seek Him, the heavens will give rain again.

"Then you will call upon Me and go and pray to Me, and I will listen to you. ***And you will seek Me and find Me, when you search for Me with all your heart."*** *(Jeremiah 29 verses 12-13, NKJV) Emphasis mine*

Pilgrims, let us keep looking for that city whose maker and builder is our God.

"for he waited for the city which has foundations, whose builder and maker is God" (Hebrews 11 verse 10)

Shall we pray?

1. Father, thank You for Your leading that is never scarce in my life. Thank You for the voice of Your spirit. Thank You for sensitivity to Your prompting. I offer You the sacrifice of my lips to praise You. Thank You because Your voice reveals the path to follow.

2. Father, I ask for forgiveness for every decision I have taken without consulting You. I repent today, let Your mercy locate me. I receive Your forgiveness and cleansing in the name of Jesus. I confess my taking actions based on logic rather than depending on Your Spirit to lead me (1 John 1 verse 9)

3. Lord, deliver me from wrong associations. Deliver me from wrong influence, deliver me from every ungodly counsel. I will not bow to pressure; I will not succumb to strange voices. As your sheep, I hear and obey Your voice only. Cause me to decipher Your voice at all times. Nudge me, prompt me always in Jesus' name

4. Lord, I will not repeat past errors concerning decisions I make. I refuse to fall into past mistakes. On every crucial matter, I wait for Your voice, Your leading comes for me, I am continually guarded by Your Spirit in Jesus' name (Psalm 32 verse 8). I acknowledge You in all my ways, please direct my path.

5. Jesus, I flow with Your plans, I yield to Your purposes, I fulfil Your mandate for me. I do nothing of myself, I

receive Your instructions in the name of Jesus. My mind, my intellect, my thoughts, my very reasoning is guided by Your Spirit in Jesus' name.

6. Lord, let my spiritual senses be receptive to Your leading and counsel. I will hear beyond the audible, I will see beyond the visible. My heart is receptive to Your will. My intellect is sharpened, I align fully with Your plans and purpose for me in Jesus' name

7. Father, I will not trade my conscience for worldly riches. My conscience will not be seared with hot iron. I refuse to be a slave to mammon. I refuse to bow before any foreign altar in the name of obtaining wealth. The deceitfulness of riches will not take me away from Your presence and Your will.

8. Jesus, You have come to give me a life of abundance, cause me to walk in the abundance of life You have for me. Grant me true riches, true honour, true joy, true wealth. Spiritually, materially, I walk in the abundance of Your provision for me. I receive in full every measure of abundance You have for me in Jesus' name.

CHAPTER FIVE

Stuck in The Mud

I had become accustomed to being chauffeur driven.
It had always been a smooth drive with my chauffeur.
To and fro on all journeys
Daily, weekly, monthly and yearly
Year in, year out it remained so
Noiseless, effortless best described our rides.
Success best depicted our daily routines; even when destinations varied.
And it was always the same story every time.
Little effort yielding maximum impact.
"Blessed" best defined our going out and coming in.
The same was applicable for all of life's endeavour
The success stories were endless!

Triumphs
Victories
Deliverances
And it flowed in again and again
Then on this fateful day, I got excited, I had received news of great success concerning an exam, I wrote earlier
A date was set for an interview

"Lord, I feel so good! I'm a genius at all I do", I thought.
So we left for the interview, chauffer driven as always
The venue was in an industrial estate
Many protocols were to be observed at the gate
Eventually we arrived at the office and as I stepped down from the back seat, I took in all around me before heading for the stairs.
"Surely a world class company"
"Must be amongst the fortune 500, I should remember to check when back home"
"Not a bad place to work at all, I hope this will sail through." I thought to myself.
Thoughts of working in this environment brought a smile
Straightening my blazer, I stepped forward
Straight to the office, I was asked to report.
Long and short was that the second stage of the interview went so well.
I came out feeling fulfilled for all had gone well.
Their best candidate for the job; so I was told.

"I just like you, Temi and I love your smile." The big boss had said to me.
Subconsciously I broke into a smile again.
"You don't just like me sir"; I thought within me;
"I carry a mark on my forehead, it's called favour."
But instead, I replied:
"Thank you sir"
And it ended, we shook hands
"By the way, see my secretary on your way out." He added
They would be contacting me in a few days
It wasn't exactly an interview in every sense of the word
More like a friendly chat
For some reason the venue seemed familiar as I headed out, like my Father owned the place.
A déjà vu feeling
That feeling
Of excitement and over confidence
Adrenalin running wild
I was on top of the world
"Made it as their best candidate." They had said
Ho! Ho!
My car pulled up just then
As I reached my car; a 2014 Lincoln Navigator SUV; my aide was on hand to hold the door open for me.
Almost unplanned, but I requested for the keys
"Are you sure you want to drive? That's what I'm here for ma'am… you really want to do this?' My chauffeur asked,

"Of course, I'm sure! I can drive, remember?"
And before he could say another word I cut in firmly
"Just give me the keys!"
My chauffer quickly took the seat beside me
I got behind the wheel and before my chauffer and aide could shut their doors, I accelerated.
Headed for the gates as we drove out of the industrial estate.
All in self-confidence, over confidence if I must say
Subtle pride in disguise.
Then at a cross road, I asked my chauffeur;
"Where do I turn?"
And before any response came, I accelerated the car and crossed the road.
Straight ahead
Out of impatience, I didn't wait for a response.
I swiftly launched forward
Then I saw it ahead, initially it appeared like a mirage; but it became clearer as we drew closer
And by then it was too late to make a diversion
There was no sign of detour either
Headlong we launched into a ditch
On a muddy path that got the car stuck
I tried reversing but only raised muddy water
I reverted to the auto cruise to move forward but tyres only screeched
No motion whatsoever
I made several efforts
All the gears failed me!

Windscreen covered in mud on all sides
We were stuck in the mud!!
I broke down, panicking, in great fear and feeling the hot tears flooding my eyes
"I should have left this driving business to this guy" I thought to myself
I turned to my chauffeur who quietly watched the scenario
I had not spared him a look since the ride began
He seemed unruffled, very unperturbed
And then He spoke to me in a sad low tone
"Temi, I have driven you all this while and we've enjoyed a jolly good ride"
"I am experienced and I know the roads better, allow me to continue driving your affairs in life. It's not about logic. Trust me, wait on me. Never jump ahead."
"I am the Holy Spirit."
And I woke up!
Sweet relief! It was just a dream.

May this forever remain a dream and never find expression in my life!
A relief and yet troubling
I was sweating profusely.
Panting like I had done a twelve story run in thirty seconds
What a dream, what an experience!
And I knew what it all meant, I needed no meditation at all.

I asked for it, I had asked Him for His counsel over a matter at the point of making a crucial decision

You see, at a point during our sojourn in Brazil; a country I had lived with my family for well over six years, I started having the urge to relocate.

My husband and I both agreed the kids were at a stage in their academics where quality education was needful as a solid base for their college admission. What better time than to act on that; but now?

Personally, I had been feeling stagnated too and itched to get back into a defined career path. I just longed for a change by that seventh year. You see, the visa type we had in Brazil restricted my getting a job.

I suspect my husband supported the idea as he often felt I had made much sacrifice following him around due to his mobile career.
"The kids and I can go back to the UK while you visit us. Lord knows we have tried here." Was my submission.

So at his approval, I sought admission for schools, for the kids and myself. Really, all was falling in place, there were interviews by Skype and telephone and then the final selections to be made
I had gained admission to do a second masters in two universities that were my first two choices. Hallelujah!

God must be in this. It's all making sense. And having fulfilled all due processes, it was time for me to apply for the UK student visa.

I was about making an appointment with the British consulate for the visa when the nudging came:
"Is this what you should be doing now?
Should this be the next move?
What is God saying about it?
A that point I looked up, heaved and decided to slow down and find out His mind.
Then I prayed. Within a week, the response came.
In the form of the incident in my dream - a warning.

I simply told my husband the dream I had and what I believed the Lord was saying to us; and we let it go.
We would stay put, together till it was God's time to relocate us Himself. Nothing like being where He wants us to be. And you know what? He gloriously moved us! Precisely two years after that incidence with much ease with a sponsored relocation.

We spent precisely nine years in that sojourn of Brazil. Nine, a number that signifies life, delivery, fruitfulness. We had arrived in Brazil in the month of July and relocated nine years after, also in the month of July.

I can still vividly remember the feeling I had on the day we left Brazil; it was all mixed up. Glad that the Lord had

finally worked out our long awaited relocation but sad to leave the country where I had experienced another level of relationship with the Lord.
As we all left for the airport in a shuttle bus, I became very emotional as my mind quickly raced through all our experiences in that land of our sojourn.

I had arrived there a cancer victim but was leaving there healed and made whole. I also recalled the initial culture shock and the language barrier we encountered. There was also the challenge with my son; we needed the Lord to help us snatch him away from the grasp of wrong influence and the Lord granted us that victory. We were also involved in little mission efforts as the Lord gave us grace in impacting the natives.

Without a doubt, in a dry and thirsty land, the Lord had preserved our spirits. He granted exemption from every perversion in the land; and in that land, I grew some "spiritual muscle" as I learnt to trust Him absolutely.

We were returning home from Brazil, not only intact; not suffering any loss, but while on our sojourn, the Lord added baby Benjamin to us!

I thought about His love, goodness and His grace that kept us all in His will and muttered within me: "Lord, thank You!"

As I turned to my husband, he said: "you are missing Brazil already, right? My wife is Brazilian at heart"

The sojourn was such a blessing! However, prior to the transfer, it was like I was going through a wilderness. I just longed for a change by all means. And in that period, I learnt a great deal from the Lord. Please permit me to share a few of my findings on passing through a wilderness and what God normally achieves in that process.

Depending on your journey, there may be lack, hunger, stagnation and or, cravings for certain needs till the Lord supplies manna and quail in that wilderness. The wilderness may not be palatable but God owns the place that seems like an entrapment. He owns the very journey of our lives. With or without subscription, wilderness experience is sure. The beauty of it was that for the children of Israel, the pillar of fire will guide by night and a cloud of glory during the day (Exodus 13 verse 21). Signifying His leading is available at such times.

"And the Lord went before them by day in a pillar of cloud to lead the way, and by night in a pillar of fire to give them light, so as to go by day and night" (Exodus 13 verse 21, NKJV)

Wilderness experiences reveal the contents of our hearts. Moses confirmed the Lord had all that 40 years tested them to reveal what was in their hearts (Deuteronomy 8 verse 2).

"And you shall remember that the Lord your God led you all the way these forty years in the wilderness, to humble you and test you, to know what was in your heart, whether you would keep His commandments or not." (Deuteronomy 8 verse 2, NKJV)

Also, God teaches His ways in the wilderness; He needed to prepare the children of Israel for that land that giants occupied. So that like Joshua and Caleb, you too can boldly say "Lord I'm ready for this next phase."

"Then Caleb quieted the people before Moses, and said, "Let us go up at once and take possession, for we are well able to overcome it." (Numbers 13 verse 30, NKJV)

Wilderness is a place of "making".
God wants our focus on Him during the wilderness and not on the journey itself. He will not remove obstacles in our way because He wants us to learn how to war by changing our perspectives on issues.

Wilderness actually shuts us in; but all for a season. And seasons are meant to "season" me. Oh! If only meat can tell the effect of heat and the 'scourging' of salt and other condiments while being cooked. But you and I can tell how delicious the meat tastes when we consume it.

Flavour is usually being added to us in the wilderness, more like an "acquisition phase".

So, what do I do?
Even in dryness and entrapment, keep your focus on Him! I can grumble and keep repeating "the same class" as in academics or I praise through till my cross over time.

Men who grumble and fall out due to difficulties never attain character formation by God because He takes time to prepare His beloved in the wilderness though the duration may vary. It`s like a waiting phase where God does some special work on His children. We must understand He places us on His schedule to spend time with Him in that waiting place. I did learn to seek God and trust Him absolutely in Brazil.

My wilderness experiences like any other must be cherished, that very training ground must be treasured because God does a deep work there.

What sustains during wilderness experiences?
Daily manna or bread from heaven as we live not by bakery baked bread alone (Mathew 4 verse 4).

"But He answered and said, "It is written, 'Man shall not live by bread alone, but by every word that proceeds from the mouth of God." (Mathew 4 verse 4)

The children of Israel had to gather manna daily and any leftover attracted worms. Manna must be special as bakery baked bread don't attract worms. And so, each morning all through that wilderness journey of 40 years, they needed to gather manna for survival.
Note that despite the fresh manna supply, not all who left Egypt or received this manna made it into the Promised Land. But only those free from complaints, murmurings and grumbling.

The right mind set, attitude and disposition at all times are needful. I must learn to trust Him even when I don't understand and just go through the process with Him.
I have learnt to simply trust and obey Him; even when nothing makes sense. (Psalm 25 verses 1 and 10)

"Unto You, O Lord, do I bring my life." (Psalm 25 verse 1, AMPC)

"All the paths of the Lord are mercy and steadfast love, even truth and faithfulness are they for those who keep His covenant and His testimonies." (Psalm 25 verse 10, AMPC)

It took a foreign voice confronting Moses through a Hebrew: *"…who made you a judge…"* (Exodus 2 verse 14) for him to run into the wilderness not realizing he was enrolling for a 40-year program.
He later became an alumnus of the "Burning Bush Graduate School". And when he came back 40 years

after, Egypt paid dearly. Certain voices will not bow in obedience till we return from the wilderness.

John the Baptist compelled a brood of vipers to repentance by virtue of his dealings from the desert. (Mathew 3 verse 7)

"But when he saw many of the Pharisees and Sadducees coming to his baptism, he said to them, "Brood of vipers! Who warned you to flee from the wrath to come? (Mathew 3 verse 7, NKJV)

Hosea learnt to hear God speak tenderly to him in the wilderness (Hosea 2 verse 14) wherein the Lord had earlier lured him.

"Therefore, behold, I will allure her, will bring her into the wilderness, and speak comfort to her." (Hosea 2 verse 14)

Ever wondered what Apostle Paul was doing in that wilderness of Arabia for 3 years? (Galatians 1) Perhaps it might have to do with his preparation for confronting that beast of Ephesus.

"nor did I go up to Jerusalem to those who were apostles before me; ***but I went to Arabia, and returned again to Damascus. Then after three years*** *I went up to Jerusalem to see Peter, and remained with him fifteen days." (Galatians 1 verse 17-18) Emphasis mine*

David knew no other life but obscurity in the bush with scorching heat while tending his papa's sheep. That was his own wilderness! He acquired skills; composing hymns, poems and love songs unto the Lord. He mastered those robe tearing dance steps. I can just picture a shepherd boy speaking animal language. From that same wilderness, his harp playing skills brought him before King Saul.

His meditative skills were so sharpened that the book of Psalm gives account of this. And he was equipped to lead God's people and mentor many. God worked on his attitude and his love waxed very strong for God. He attained wisdom and comportment in dealing with offenses.

It was a time of deep and intense waiting but he eventually came forth. When he had passed all his tests and his time of showing came forth, that flask of pressed olive oil bulged and automatically popped open at his presence without further hesitation (1 Samuel 16); signifying one who had passed the wilderness test and the resulting reward was his enthronement both as king and as a prophet unto God.

When you graduate from the wilderness school, it will be obvious. Your approval will be evident to all. We must recognise times and seasons. You are not forgotten; you will not remain obscure. You will rise above mediocrity and you will not be overcome. No matter what phase you are in that wilderness sojourn, you are coming out and coming out big. Men will speak in your favour. The dark days will be over and kings will come to your rising. You will be favoured, you will be great and all eyes shall see.

Just go through it for God owns the journey. We therefore receive grace to walk in the light of His leading always.

Would you heartily pray over these points?

1. Lord, I enter Your gates with praises today. I celebrate You my Maker and my God. The Lover of my soul, the Bishop of my life, the Captain of my salvation, thank You for being involved in all my affairs. I am grateful for all You do in my life. Thank You for Your faithfulness and tender mercies over me. Take all the glory in Jesus' name.

2. Thank You for diverse victories, triumphs, deliverances and success in all endeavours. Thank You for Your favour all round. Thank You for Your numerous blessings that are uncountable. You are the source of every blessing. Thank You for ease on all sides. Glory be to Your holy name.

3. Today, I repent of any pride, high mindedness or acts of overconfidence. Truly, it is not by power nor by might but by Your Spirit. I repent of any act where I had tried to take the wheel of my life off Your hands or called the shots myself. Please forgive me, wash me thoroughly in Jesus' name.

4. Holy Spirit, I rededicate my life again, fill me, lead me, guide me, rebuke me, counsel me, help me, deliver me, reveal the Word to me, transform me, inspire me, stir me, teach me, bring all things to my remembrance. I hand over my life to You, please lead me and I will follow.

5. In aspects where I had gotten into error due to my impatience, Father recover me, restore me, make seasons and times to work in my favour. You have the times and seasons in Your hands, help me to regain lost times and seasons. Grant me speed on every side in Jesus' name.

6. Father, I lay all my plans at Your feet, let Your will be known, let Your will be done. Let me be moved only by Your word. Cause my reasoning to align with Your plan & purpose in Jesus' name. I make no move where Your Spirit does not lead me in Jesus' name.

7. As a family, we walk in unity of purpose under the guidance of the Holy Spirit. We follow Your precepts, Your Spirit guides us always. Every aspect of our lives is guided by You in Jesus' name

8. Lord, through every wilderness experience, let me feed on Your Word. Let Your manna be enough for me. Send Your Word to me per time and season. Let the pillar of fire guide me by night and the cloud of glory guide me by the day. Make Your word a lamp unto my feet and a light unto my path. Thank you Father!

CHAPTER SIX

A Child's Outcry

The year was 2008 and it was only the second day in the New Year.

It was one of those cold winter mornings in Aberdeen.

My husband was travelling so I was alone at home with the kids.

I raised my head to check the time.

It was around 5 a.m. in the morning.

"Time to pray" I thought to myself

I didn't particularly have a restful night and so I wanted to sleep a little longer.

The cold was just too conducive for more slumber.

School and work resumption was the very next day. I might as well sleep a little longer.

I pulled the thick duvet over me again.
And just as I was settling in to sleep
It came
Oh! That voice
Like a sound of many waters
Thunderous . . .
Furious, momentous, grave
It flooded my ear and I heard beyond the audible
Fierce, firm and serious
Like a warning, it roared and echoed
Weighty . . .
First in an unknown tongue
Which I did not understand
And then I heard it
"Claim your shield rights! Claim your shield rights!!"
Like a stern warning
Coupled with a firm advice
Or more like an urgent order
It sounded like all of it to me!
Eyes flung open
Cold seem to have melted away at that voice
Sleep departed like it was never there
I ruminated over those words
Shield, rights, claim . . .
Surely, shield must be connected with faith, it happens to be one of the components of the armour of God described by Apostle Paul in Ephesians 6

And rights must be something I'm entitled to, perhaps it was being contested for so I needed to claim it back? Or, I was to enforce something that is lawfully mine.
"What is the essence of the shield from scriptures?" I pondered

"above all, taking the shield of faith with which you will be able to quench all the fiery darts of the wicked one." (Ephesians 6 verse 16)

Basically, to quench fiery darts of the devil
Fiery darts were attacks to come. Hmm! This will be a very glorious year
Highly consequential in a new year.
And to imagine I had been asking the Lord for a word for 2008. I somehow interpreted that scripture to mean if my shield of faith were lifted high enough before me, there will be divine empowerment to fight against and extinguish every single fiery dart the devil will ever try to send my way!
A year of quenching fiery darts.
I got up to pray immediately
And prayed I did.
The year had a lot of unfolding to do. A very interesting year it was for me.
I was unprepared for what unfolded but thankfully, the Lord had gone ahead of me.
A couple of weeks into the year, we had this grave concern that my daughter who was just under five years

old may have had a medical condition that was affecting her kidneys and bladder.
And so, the school recommended that we consulted a General Practitioner. We got an appointment secured with the General Practitioner and on the visit, tests were requested and done.

The results came out that all was well with all her organs.
Her bladder and kidneys were certified okay.
The laboratory results revealed all was normal.
But the condition persisted.
The first week gave way to the second week and then to the third.
At this point, worry set in.
We put all physical checks and balances humanly possible in place but the situation failed to improve.
By the end of the third week, I began to despair.
I requested for another set of tests to be done
Again, results came back revealing nothing

In retrospect, the search within began
What could be happening?
Was there something the doctors weren't seeing?
So we turned it over to the Lord in prayers. For some reason, there was peace within. Having prayed through, we just decided to stand and wait for His salvation, restful in Him.
Faith has many facets, being restful after seeking God is one of them. Yes, faith can be restful.

Scripture admonishes us to stand having done all.

"Therefore take up the whole armour of God, that you may be able to withstand in the evil day, and having done all, to stand" (Ephesians 6:13 NKJV)

Just like that word I had received earlier instructing me to claim my shield rights, the full armour of God was to be in place, this included an active faith. Faith must not be bound. The need to have a faith that is alive is a major requirement in order to quench every fiery dart of the devil. I needed that faith to withstand in those days.

So, having prayed and believed God, the only thing left was to rest in Him. Believing He would correct whatever needs to be done in my daughter.
We prayed over her daily and injected faith words in her.
She was told her Jesus would heal her.
And all this while, my husband was in and out of town on official assignment.
Whenever we spoke, he would ask:
"How far? Any improvement?"
"It is well." Was my response consistently
On one Saturday afternoon she ran to me in the kitchen wailing
"Mummy, will Jesus not heal me? When will it stop? I'm tired mommy."
Stooping low next to her I responded

"Bibi, Jesus will heal you, only He can. We just have to trust Him to do it. It will happen when only He knows but I know He will do it, okay? He really loves you and cares about this. Just trust Him, okay?"
I looked into her face reassuringly, dried her tears and then we prayed together.
Having, done all, we just stood by faith, waiting for God's salvation. Restful that God would show up for her.

Ask me as a responsible parent if there wasn't more I could have done? Sincerely, we just rested in God. Not because we were not concerned for our child; but because we had learnt to lay everything at His feet in the place of prayer.
Yes, faith can be restful.

The fourth week ended and so did the fifth week.
Though, I cannot specifically say when; that mysterious occurrence fizzled out exactly the way it came. It must have lasted between six and seven weeks. But I remember vividly we thanked God and gave her a befitting 5th birthday.

Suffice to highlight at this point that having received that word from God on the need to "claim my shield rights" which is faith in this case, a Christian soldier equips himself or herself with the full armour of God and not just one or two. They all work together, for a soldier cannot go to war with only a shield. The girdle of truth which is integrity, the sword of the Spirit which is God's Word, the breastplate of righteousness which talks about the righteous standing we have in Christ and all other parts of the armour must be in place.

Bible knowledge is not enough; for anybody can quote scriptures. We actually need the Holy Spirit who is the Author of the Word in using the sword of the Spirit which is the Word of God. We cannot separate the Word from the other components of the armour because all of them work together.
The Word of God in Philippians 4 verse 6 translated our family to that phase of rest.

"Be anxious for nothing, but in everything by prayer and supplication, with thanksgiving, let your requests be made known to God;" (Philippians 4 verse 6, NKJV)

Precisely two months after her birthday, I had need again to use that shield of faith in quenching another fiery dart of the devil targeted at me this time.

Dear reader, I have come to the conclusion that it isn't fate, but faith, that determines how we handle unfolding events in our lives. Our hopes must be built continually on things eternal, firmly hinged like an anchor on God`s unfailing promises.

We had celebrated our daughter's birthday on the 1st of March and the 1st of May, I witnessed an attack that jolted my family for the next nine months in that same year. It was the genesis of ovarian cancer that tested the effectiveness of that shield of faith, a shield that by His grace I had learnt to claim and maximize in quenching every fiery darts of the devil.

Details of that testimony of that attack and how the Lord gave me victory was fully shared in my first book titled **Not a Stranger to Storms**; a story of God's faithfulness. A God that defends and honors His Word in the lives of His children. He is just too faithful to fail, full of compassion and mercy.

Sincerely, faith is a shield and an important component of God's armor every believer must arm themselves with if victory is to be obtained in every battle of life. It answers always and never fails. When applied with full understanding, it is never a risk. The devil will always throw darts in this life's sojourn and that's okay. In other words, it is okay as a believer to face trials and challenges but the gospel truth is that we should not be defeated, that is not God's desire for any of His children.

"For whatever is born of God overcomes the world. And this is the victory that has overcome the world—our faith." (1 John 5 verse 4)

By faith we overcome all of the devil's whims. There is an assurance that God answers prayers. That assurance is intertwined with faith. And faith is the currency for withdrawing from the bank of heaven.

If truly God answers prayers, why do some petitions, supplications and intercessions go unanswered? Did I hear anyone say "especially when asked according to His will?" It might be due to certain little foxes.

So stop me if you are familiar with any of these:
Ever paid attention to your thoughts? I mean unguarded thoughts. The thoughts going on in your mind; the thoughts you permit in your mind after praying over a matter are important to faith yielding results

"Keep your heart with all diligence, for out of it spring the issues of life." (Proverbs 4 verse 23 NKJV)

The thoughts I permit, the activities in my mind after praying reveal the real me.

"For as he thinketh in his heart so is he" (Proverbs 23 verse7 NKJV.)

From my input of thoughts flows the outcome of my life. God responds to the words of my mouth as well as the thoughts going on in my mind. He works with the thoughts in our mind!

*"**But without thy mind would I do nothing**; that thy benefit should not be as it were of necessity, but willingly." (Philemon 1 verse 14 KJV) Emphasis mine*

We must consciously guard our hearts and watch what thoughts we permit when we believe God for anything by faith. The mind must be tightened to make no room for doubts.

*"**Therefore gird up the loins of your mind**, be sober, and rest your hope fully upon the grace that is to be brought to you at the revelation of Jesus Christ;" (1Pet 1verse 13 NKJV) Emphasis mine*

Our thoughts are as powerful as our prayers. God answers to our prayers as well as our thoughts.

*"**Now to Him who is able to do exceedingly abundantly above all that we ask or think,** according to the power that works in us" (Ephesians 3 verse 20) Emphasis mine*

"That you ask or think" implies God answers our thinking too!

*"Let the **words of my mouth** and the **meditation of my heart**. Be acceptable in Your sight, O Lord, my strength and my Redeemer." (Psalm 19 verse 14 NKJV) Emphasis mine*

So, my prayer can be cancelled by my thinking; because praying correctly and then thinking wrongly will yield nothing because one, take away one equals to zero.
I must pray well and according to His will; but also importantly, I need to think well.
There are arguments in our minds that need casting down as well as every high thing that exalts itself against the knowledge of God. We need to consciously bring every thought into captivity to the obedience of Christ.

*"For though we walk in the flesh, we do not war according to the flesh. For the weapons of our warfare are not carnal but mighty in God for pulling down strongholds, **casting down arguments and every high thing that exalts itself against the knowledge of God, bringing every thought into captivity to the obedience of Christ"** (2 Corinthians 10 verses 3-5 NKJV) Emphasis mine*

Secondly, a believer that will truly claim the shield of faith must beware of double mindedness. Doubting implies instability like the waves of the sea and the only guarantee it offers is not receiving anything from the Lord.

"But let him ask in faith, with no doubting, for he who doubts is like a wave of the sea driven and tossed by the wind. For let not that man suppose that he will receive anything from the Lord; he is a double-minded man, unstable in all his ways." (James 1verse 6-8)

Be reminded that it is possible to cancel one's supplication, intercessions or answers to prayers when one gives room to doubt. The devil may not be perturbed that I pray because he can still try to hinder me through my thoughts. He would do everything to quench my faith so it produces no result.
Again, we must lay to heart that it is pertinent that we believe God absolutely;

"For assuredly, I say to you, whoever says to this mountain, 'Be removed and be cast into the sea,' ***and does not doubt in his heart, but believes that those things he says will be done, he will have whatever he says."*** *(Mark 11 verse 23) Emphasis mine*

Doubting God's Words in our hearts hinders results. God answers both expectations and meditations, it therefore suggests that right expectation plus right thinking is the "access code" we need as a guarantee to receiving answers from the Lord. We must learn to believe God absolutely.

So, permit me at this point to tie the faith subject up in a "neat bow" with the focus of this book. It would seem this dimension makes the faith walk much fun!

Having realized that faith is an ever winning spiritual force, how does it come? How do I grow it? How do I maintain the potency of my faith in the face of challenging circumstances?

Faith comes by hearing.
"So then faith comes by hearing, and hearing by the word of God" (Romans 10 verse 17 NKJV) Emphasis mine

It is not out of place to say that faith comes by hearing from God directly. Each time the Lord spoke to me, it cleared every doubt. Each time the Lord rebuked me, I sat up straight.
Each time the Lord speaks to me, I can be rest assured if I follow what He says, He's committed to backing me up and guaranteed results would be the outcome. Nothing births boldness and audacity like hearing from God!

I will cite a few examples from scriptures and some of God's gracious dealings with me.

At the age of 75, it took faith for Abraham to depart from his father's house to a land which the Lord promised to show him. I mean, who does that?

"Now the Lord had said to Abram: "Get out of your country, From your family
And from your father's house, to a land that I will show you. I will make you a great nation; I will bless you and make your name great; and you shall be a blessing. I will bless those who bless you, and I will curse him who curses you;

*And in you all the families of the earth shall be blessed." **So Abram departed as the Lord had spoken to him**, and Lot went with him." (Genesis 12 verse 1-4) Emphasis mine*

The voice of God that Abraham heard directly gingered his faith to embark on that journey to the unknown. He wasn't given a forwarding address of which country it would be, but he upped and went! Such height of faith!

When Moses returned to Egypt for the deliverance of the Israelites, it was like coming to dare Egypt; a country he fled from. But he could do that because he heard God. What gave a stammerer and murderer the boldness and the effrontery to confront Pharaoh? After a long conversation with I AM THAT I AM, Moses obtained boldness. The resultant faith that came from hearing God!

***"Come now, therefore, and I will send you to Pharaoh that you may bring My people, the children of Israel, out of Egypt**." But Moses said to God, "Who am I that I should go to Pharaoh, and that I should bring the children of Israel out of Egypt?" So He said, "I will certainly be with you. And this shall be a sign to you that I have sent you: When you have brought the people out of Egypt, you shall serve God on this mountain." Then Moses said to God, "Indeed, when I come to the children of Israel and say to them, 'The God of your fathers has sent me to you,' and they say to me, 'What is His name?' what shall I say to them?" And God said to Moses, "I AM*

WHO I AM." And He said, "Thus you shall say to the children of Israel, 'I AM has sent me to you.'" Moreover, God said to Moses, "Thus you shall say to the children of Israel: 'The Lord God of your fathers, the God of Abraham, the God of Isaac, and the God of Jacob, has sent me to you. This is My name forever, and this is My memorial to all generations. (Exodus 3 verse 10-14) Emphasis mine

Hearing God for ourselves infuses a potent faith that can never be shaken. Accessibility to God's voice gives audacity. The height of Moses' boldness came when He heard God say to him that He has been made as a God to Pharaoh!

***"So the Lord said to Moses: "See, I have made you as God to Pharaoh**, and Aaron your brother shall be your prophet." (Exodus 7 verse 1) Emphasis mine*

The voice of God is all we need to hear in settling every doubt in life.
When the financial situation was tough during the time Isaac dwelt amongst the Philistines, he had the option of going down to Egypt where the economy must have been very buoyant but as he sought God, direction came for Him and the Lord reassured Him He would bless Him in that very land where dryness was prevalent.

"There was a famine in the land, besides the first famine that was in the days of Abraham. And Isaac went to Abimelech king

of the Philistines, in Gerar. Then the Lord appeared to him and said: "Do not go down to Egypt; live in the land of which I shall tell you. Dwell in this land, and I will be with you and bless you; for to you and your descendants I give all these lands, and I will perform the oath which I swore to Abraham your father. And I will make your descendants multiply as the stars of heaven; I will give to your descendants all these lands; and in your seed all the nations of the earth shall be blessed; because Abraham obeyed My voice and kept My charge, My commandments, My statutes, and My laws." So Isaac dwelt in Gerar." (Genesis 26 verse 1-6)

In the midst of all the hardship, Isaac obeyed God by faith and dwelt in that dry land. It took Isaac hearing directly for sustaining faith to keep him in that land. In that same year, His obedience by faith to God's word was rewarded.

"Then Isaac sowed in that land, and reaped in the same year a hundredfold; and the Lord blessed him. The man began to prosper, and continued prospering until he became very prosperous;" (Genesis 26 verse 12-13)

How about the Apostles in the book of Acts? A time came when their faith became so bold. Their tenacity in preaching the gospel became contagious because they heard from God, they had experienced Jesus first hand. They became unstoppable!

"For we cannot but speak the things which we have seen ***and heard****." (Acts 4:20) Emphasis mine*

The Apostles individually heard and that was what fired them up to go declare Christ boldly. There was a hearing and a seeing in their case. So nothing could move them when they received threats to stop preaching in the name of Jesus.

It is convincing enough to say that the heroes of faith listed in Hebrews chapter 11 all heard God at one point or the other. An encounter with His voice must have fired up faith in them to believe God absolutely.

Dear reader, God still speaks today, I stand as a living witness. When you have access to that Voice over matters in your life, challenging situations melt away.

I will summarize this encounter. However; the full details can be found in the chapter 6 of my first book titled ***"Not A Stranger to Storms"***.

We had been faced with a situation where we needed the Lord to help us snatch our first son away from the pangs of wrong influence in a strange land. My heart was bleeding as a mother and surely, no living soul could help. As parents, we were almost concluding it was best I relocated with the children in a bid to cut off the wrong influences on our child.

One morning in autumn, I decided to seek God over the matter. So I entered my room while everyone was out. I just needed to hear from God in that overwhelming situation. I must have been languishing in prayer like Hannah at Shiloh with great sorrow. My heart was truly connected, I didn't have to wait for long, Exodus 3 verse 12 was dropped in my spirit and as I opened to read, the words lifted before my face.

"So He said, "I will certainly be with you. And this shall be a sign to you that I have sent you: When you have brought the people out of Egypt, ***you shall serve God on this mountain"*** *(Exodus 3 verse 12) Emphasis mine*

All I could hear God saying was on this same mountain you will worship Me. He was set to contend with every contention and save my son.

At these words, I broke out in a smile. I knew I wasn't to move anywhere for any reason. I went into that room to pray a dejected soul but came out a different person entirely; a bold lioness. He had assured me of His presence being with me, and in that very place, He said I would worship Him. What more can I ask for than His presence? With faith fired up from that moment, I rested in Him and indeed He was glorified.

This particular 6th chapter of the book ***"Not A Stranger to Storms"*** explains how we can fully trust God to fight our battles. It comes highly recommended for parents having challenges or crisis at some point in child upbringing. His promise to us remains that He would contend with them that contend with us and that He would save our children.

Friends, faith resolves every issue in life and I have seen it work in all areas of my life

"But thus says the Lord: "Even the captives of the mighty shall be taken away, And the prey of the terrible be delivered; ***For I will contend with him who contends with you, And I will save your children."*** *(Isaiah 49 verse 25) Emphasis mine*

Oh! He did show up over that matter, praise God!

On another occasion, I was confronted with a medical report of multiple fibroid and that possibility of conception was next to no existence. God in His humorous way had visited me, I took in that very month, almost 13 years after the last conception. As I visited the doctor to notify her of my pregnancy, she nearly drowned my faith out with her insistence that it wasn't possible.

As she sat in front of me speaking, the visitations I had where the Lord spoke about the baby and even gave some details concerning the unborn child made me break out in a smile right before this female practitioner.

If only she knew what I knew. If only she heard what I had heard. If only she saw what the Lord showed me. Too late for her words, faith had been received over this matter.

There was another encounter I experienced when there the Spirit of God interrupted me during my personal worship and spoke to me about the coming year with respect to a loved one. God sent a warning ahead that a great shaking was coming but that this dear person to me would not be affected. Truly, the following year was quaky for this friend, even my very person would have been shaken at the happenings that following year. But for God's revealed voice that served as an anchor and saw us through; it would have been devastating!

God speaks via His word and we bear in mind that behind every scripture is God's voice. When the Spirit leads you to such words in scripture, it just comes alive to you.

Faith is an adventure in God and one that is always rewarded by God so, how can I be helped in growing mine?
It's basically about hearing and recognizing that voice. That voice that brings guidance and makes the inexperienced operate in the same class as the learned. That voice that is fundamental to fulfillment in all

endeavors. He speaks but we must tune in to receive from Him.

We must recognize that tuning in is another word for walking in the Spirit. I have a particular radio station I love to listen to while driving. So, once I start driving, I just search for that station and tune in to listen.

"If we live in the Spirit, ***let us also walk in the Spirit."*** *(Galatians 5 verse 25) Emphasis mine*

While it calls for being sensitive to the dictates of the Spirit in our daily walk, we must consciously engage in a lifestyle of praise.

"You shall have a song as in the night when a holy festival is kept, and gladness of heart as when one goes with a flute, to come into the mountain of the Lord, To the Mighty One of Israel" (Isaiah 30 verse 29, NKJV)

A song signifies worship, a praiseful attitude. We easily access His voice when we have a song. The same was used by the prophet Elisha. He called for singers

"Then Elisha said to the king of Israel, "What have I to do with you? Go to the prophets of your father and the prophets of your mother." But the king of Israel said to him, "No, for the Lord has called these three kings together to deliver them into the hand of Moab." And Elisha said, "As the Lord of hosts lives,

before whom I stand, surely were it not that I regard the presence of Jehoshaphat king of Judah, I would not look at you, nor see you. 15 ***But now bring me a musician." Then it happened, when the musician played, that the hand of the Lord came upon him. 16 And he said, "Thus says the Lord: 'Make this valley full of ditches.'*** *(2 Kings 3 verse 13 – 16 NKJV) Emphasis mine*

The voice of the Lord came in the form of His hand resting upon Elisha after the minstrels sang. Their praise and worship brought down God's presence. In those days the Holy Spirit only descended and ascended on prophets. It was only after the day of Pentecost that the Spirit of God began to indwell in every true believer. A consistent lifestyle of praise and worship ensures regular access to the voice of the Spirit of God that dwells within us.

Again, a lifestyle of prayer and fasting should not be ignored but must be a regular program in the life of a believer.

"But you, when you pray, *go into your room, and when you have shut your door, pray to your Father who is in the secret place; and your Father who sees in secret will reward you openly." (Mathew 6 verse 6 NKJV) Emphasis mine*

"But you, when you fast, *anoint your head and wash your face" (Matthew 6 verse 17 NKJV) Emphasis mine*

Please note that in both scriptures, it is a case of "when you pray" and "when you fast" and not the conditional "if you pray" or "if you fast". And so, praying and fasting are obligatory, not optional for a believer that yearns to hear God's voice.

Prayer exposes me more to the aura of God or endears me more to His presence while fasting helps put the flesh under so the voice of the Spirit can be better heard. The faith realm requires that we learn how to stand upon our watch in order to hear.

"I will stand my watch and set myself on the rampart, and watch to see what He will say to me, and what I will answer when I am corrected." (Habakkuk 2 verse 1)

Standing upon my watch in prayers, fasting, worship and consistently being sensitive to His leading makes me one that learns how to be present with the Lord always. A diligent search of the truth on any subject matter that is of interest to us is important. God has been known to speak through materials of His prophets as expressed in the book of Hosea 12.

***"I have also spoken by the prophets**, and have multiplied visions; I have given symbols [b]through the witness of the prophets" (Hosea 12 verse 10 NKJV) Emphasis mine*

I choose to add my voice by saying that every believer should strive to hear directly from God. While He plants certain prophets in our paths that they may confirm what He has spoken to us. Many have however, hidden behind scriptures like this to depend on the ministry of prophets concerning every decision of guidance for their lives.

God desires to speak to you directly. The same way you have physical senses to hear, taste and see, our spiritual senses can also be developed to receive from the throne room of heaven.

When you hear directly from God, faith is fired up! Faith resolves all issues of life. I have seen God move practically in all areas of life. I've seen God manifest in strange ways.
Remember, it is to every man according to His faith.

Let us pray

1. Father, in the name of Jesus. I want to celebrate You for counting me amongst the beloved. Thank You for that banner of love over me, thank You for sonship, thank You for access, thank You for revelation. I'm grateful because You love me so much. You correct me because You desire that I conform to Your image of holiness.

2. Lord today, I openly confess I have erred in so many ways and gone contrary to Your instructions. Father, please forgive every act of faithlessness in my life. I specifically ask that You forgive me in every way I have doubted You.

3. Lord I pray that no matter what You permit to come my way, I overcome them all in the name of Jesus. Help me to find rest; Your Word says there remains a rest for the people of God, I find that rest and I enter into it in Jesus' name. Like the Hebrew children, I come out of any and every fiery furnace ten times better.

4. I declare in the name of Jesus that I am an overcomer, I am born of You, I have victory in all circumstances, I prevail always, I win always. No matter what, situations end to my benefit. I am more than a conqueror through You that loved me.

5. Lord, I receive grace to seek You always. In fasting, in prayer, in worship, in diligent search of Your Word. As I stand upon my watch regularly, send Your word my way. Give me a regular encounter with You in Jesus' name. I grow from faith to faith in the name of Jesus.

6. Lord, today, I ask that every scale fall off my eyes, every veil be torn off my heart, every blockage be removed from my ears. I hear You clearly, I see visions and revelations. You speak clearly to my heart in the

name of Jesus. My entire spiritual senses are all alive and sensitive to receive from You in Jesus' name.

7. Lord, increase my faith, help my unbelief. As You speak to me, grant me understanding. As I hear You let wisdom come. When You speak to my heart, cause me to be receptive. As I study Your Word diligently, let insight come in the name of Jesus.

8. Jesus, I thank You. I am persuaded that much more than I ask or imagine You will do in my life. In my faith walk, thank You for growth, thank You for great faith and exceeding great faith. I celebrate Your work in my life. In Jesus' name.

CHAPTER SEVEN

The Headlights

The months of October till March are typically hot in Brazil. This period typifies the summer season. Verao, as called in Portuguese is a season much loved by the Brazilians as it encourages much of outdoor activities. As a way of life, Brazilians enjoy eating out, the beaches were patronized by all and sundry, the heat was always at its peak. This was a time when every household maximized the use of their swimming pools, big or small, and lots of barbeque was the order of the day during this season.

Shopping malls were typically jam packed with people; not out for shopping but out to escape the heat in their homes while they walked around. They stopped by at shops to snack, most just sauntered around with ice cream, candy or a drink in hand. I had often wondered if some of the window shopping was not an attempt to reduce the use of air conditioning during the day in their homes and subsequently, reduction in electricity bills.

The year 2009 had Verao arriving much earlier, more like an unwanted guest for me as it marked periods of higher perspiration and the arrival of tiny flying and biting insects. As early as September of that year, the heat had become scorching. Perhaps the global warming was visiting Brazil specially. It was during this period that I felt strongly that the Lord was asking for a meeting to reach out to a certain class of people within the community where we lived.

Having discussed with my husband, we braced up for that, set a date and then preparations began in earnest. I envisaged thirty invites would be sent out.
An outreach to the expatriate community.
And then it occurred to me to ask what the message should be specifically.
So I asked in prayer and waited.
And waited.

Till it was almost 3 days to the set date and yet, nothing was laid on my heart. Invitations were already out. I could share with people that came on many topics but I

desired to know what God had in mind for that meeting since He initiated it.
Just two days before that Friday night meeting, something interesting happened that changed my perspective about listening and waiting for God's voice. I set out for a ride to the post office at the city centre. It was not my usual route; neither was visiting the city centre my thing. It was always busy and car parking was a herculean task during the week.

This was a Wednesday morning and I needed to pick a parcel from the post office. I opted to dash there and back early enough; but not too early as rush hour traffic wasn't my thing either. However, early enough to avoid the sun's heat permeating. The weather had promised a bright sunny day. So I set out at about 9.30am that fateful morning.

As I drove along, I was humming to the song of a renowned Nigerian gospel artist by the name, Wale Adenuga. I hummed and danced along to the track; "This is not enough" from the car CD player. I sure love this artist, He always had a way of connecting me easily with worship.

Traffic was light for that time of the day and I was moving within reasonable speed for that particular road and I couldn't help but notice an oncoming vehicle from the other direction flashing the car lights. I ignored the first two flash light warnings. Then, another came, flashed and horned. Subsequent ones passed by without any warning. That brought a kind of relief.

And then another came, flashing again and again.
"Wait a minute, can something be wrong with my car?"
"Is there a robbery ahead on this road?"
"Oh! Maybe an accident?"
"Surely, it can't be traffic ahead! Not at this time of the day."
"A road block maybe? Well, if they made it, so would I."
I thought within me

I reaffirmed to myself that I had checked the car before leaving the house, everything was fine. My husband used the car over the weekend and he would have detected if anything was wrong. A quick glance at the dash board reassured me all was well. It's a relatively new car anyway. Nothing could possibly be wrong.

There can't possibly be robbery on this road; a police station was less than a mile away. If it's an accident, I will just drive slowly. I was closer to my destination anyway. So, I continued, humming to another song. And then, another car came, flashing.

And just before I could react, the road block ahead became visible. There was a narrow path open for cars to pass by. I noticed a truck loaded with two cars, other cars parked by the road side and a slow moving traffic from both directions. There were uniformed men in brown; they were impounding cars that were not yet certified as road worthy for the year. Those who had registered for the test as well as those who already took the test were exempted.

For a minute, I panicked. But I remembered I had handed the car documents to my husband a while back to book the test. I however never followed up afterwards. I was still confident all was well as I awaited my turn to be inspected by the officer. Surely, I can't be a victim.

It was too late to start rummaging for car documents to confirm anyway and I trust my husband would have taken care of it.

When it got to my turn, the officer simply looked at their radar and said to me in Portuguese,
"Senhora, please clear out of the way. From our records, your car has not been certified road worthy for the year. We will have to impound your car!"

In retrospect now, we had paid the annual fees but neither my husband nor myself knew we were supposed to take the car for inspection as it was purchased new.
What a way to learn!
Costly ignorance

We were still very new in the system.
He spoke with such authority and in a formal tone.
I knew it was final.
And he walked off to the next car. All my efforts to try explain in my little Portuguese that it wasn't possible and that I was certain my husband took care of it fell on deaf ears.

As I moved the car to the side of the road, I placed a call to my husband.
"Guess where I am"
"Where?" He answered
"I'm being held for not running road worthiness test, we needed to have booked the car for a test aside paying the annual fees"
"I remember you asked me for the documents way back"
I left it hanging
"We just never knew. After all, I effected payment for the annual fees. We were ignorant of the need for inspection." He simply responded
"Where exactly are you?" He then added
"Let me get someone who speaks their language well and we will meet up with you."
I described my exact location.
Before he could make it down to the location with a friend, my car had been assembled with other cars on the trailer. We watched as my car was taken away along with five other cars.

We arrived at their office. A lot of bureaucracy was involved. They just didn't seem to be in a hurry. The officials took their time, oblivious of us all.
It's not their fault anyway. I should have paid attention to such things. It would have simply been easier to register and get the road worthiness test done.
I resolved to take personal responsibility for this henceforth. After all, it was just once in a year.
And so we had to move from one office to another.
A process involving many long queues.
With impoundment documents at hand, proof of penalty payment effected, we immediately booked online for the road worthiness test. Thereafter, we drove to the suburbs to pick my car after providing all documentations.

By the time we recovered the car, it was all covered in dust. I quickly dashed to a car wash and finally headed home in order to arrive before the kids returned from school.

As I entered the house, I shut the door and leaned back on it with my hands and head resting on the door.
Lord, what a day!
Even with the car air conditioning, the heat of the day had really dealt with me. I could do with a cold shower.
Then it occurred to me; I didn't even make it to the post office.
And then I knew it; like an idea, all was coming together.
And that imagination formed before me.

"Friday message well received".
As if the Lord was saying I needed that experience to deliver accurately at the outreach meeting slated for Friday night.

Suddenly, it all began to make sense: they need to know that You are flashing headlights at them with this message. Many other such messages had been flashed by other carriers of the gospel and avenues of preaching this message to them from colleagues at work or even the voice of their consciences. Just because they enjoy comfort, good health, ride good cars with beautiful houses does not mean all is well with their souls. In this case, it will be too late to recover.

I must explain what God's salvation plan is. And that they need to be sure they are certified citizens of His kingdom. They should heed all signs now; no ignorance was acceptable as excuse.
Before it is too late.
For there will be a day of reckoning
No escaping such
And it will be when it is least expected
I quickly got a pen.
My face lit for a minute and all the tiredness and frustration of the day suddenly waned off!
The Friday meeting came and passed and great was the impact thereof.
All glory to His name

